THE ZODIAC AND THE SOUL

THE ZODIAC AND THE SOUL

By

C. E. O. CARTER

ASTROLOGY CLASSICS
207 VICTORY LANE, BEL AIR MD 21014

On the cover: The piano teacher looks towards home, Iola, March 1971. Photograph by David R. Roell

Photo of Charles Carter found in the 1972 printing of Astrological Aspects

ISBN 978 1 933303 33 8

This edition published 2010

Published by
Astrology Classics

the publication division of
The Astrology Center of America
207 Victory Lane, Bel Air MD 21014

on line at www.**AstroAmerica.com**

CONTENTS

FOREWORD

ABOUT a year ago I wrote a small book entitled "The Seven Great Problems of Astrology". In it I attempted to break the ground, as it were, for the discussion of some of the deeper aspects of our science, and in doing so I confess that I expected no very general response. To my surprise this little work sold freely, and some critics, notably a writer in *Modern Astrology*, were particularly encouraging.

The present book is written in somewhat the same vein. It is designed to interest those who share with the writer a certain point of view, of which the chief characteristic is a belief that the material world is a reflection of an ideal world and that man subsists in an intermediate condition, linking the one with the other, and turning his face, like Janus, in two directions.

Those who have no sympathy with such a mode of thought I will try to placate in due course with more immediately practical work, but in the meanwhile I hope that some congenial souls will enjoy parts at least of these Discourses.

One merry gentleman found fault with the "Seven Problems" on the grounds that there was *too much reason in it*. But Astrology is the reason or significance of the Stars, and it is their real meaning that is of value to some of us, even more than the peculiarities of temperament and destiny with which they are associated in particular horoscopes. Having obtained a knowledge of general astrological principles, we can deal safely and surely with particular instances, and this constitutes true practical astrology rather than a mere empiric observation of a few maps. I believe that most astrologers, both now and in past ages, have taken this view.

September 1928   CHARLES E. O. CARTER

NOTE TO SECOND EDITION

Most of the alterations in this new edition of a work first published eighteen years ago are of a purely verbal character, designed to clarify the meaning of the text.

In Chapter Three I have, however, abandoned the attempt to correlate the Planets with the Seven Cosmic Planes, a task which has been difficult ever since the discovery of Uranus and, with the advent of Neptune and Pluto, to say nothing of the Planetoids, has become almost impossible.

I have also excised all references to the so-called solar epoch introduced by W. H. Sampson, believing it to be of very dubious validity.

C. E. O. CARTER

1947

NOTE TO THIRD EDITION

In the Third Edition I have added a chapter on Transits, feeling as I do that this is a subject that has not received the attention that it merits, at least so far as the written word is concerned.

Further, there is an additional chapter upon the possibilities of applying true numerology or the lore of numbers to the horoscope. This I believe to be original, and, while my suggestions may lead some into the morass of fantasy, I think that those who avoid this temptation and keep their feet firmly on the ground may discover things well worth knowing.

C. E. O. CARTER

1960

I

THE DERIVATION OF THE TWELVE

MUCH has been written about the Zodiac, and from many points of view.

To the astronomer it is merely the pathway of the Sun, the Moon, and the planets, possessing no more reality than the tracks of liners shown upon an atlas for the information of the intending traveller. To him the division of the circle into twelve signs and 360 degrees is equally arbitrary, and he naïvely attributes the names of the signs to a fancied resemblance between certain animals and the constellations which at one time coincided with Aries, Taurus, and the rest, though they do so no more. Unrestrained indeed must have been the imagination which saw a likeness between the constellation Cancer and any crab known to man, between Libra and a balance, or, in fact, between any of the twelve and the entities of which they bear the names, with the possible exceptions of Aries, Taurus, and Leo. Gemini, also, might reasonably be supposed to have received its name from the twin stars Castor and Pollux.

But to the astrologer the Zodiac is a real thing, even if he cannot see or feel it in physical sense.[1] He knows that it is

---

[1] I believe that a sensitive person could, with practice, learn actually to feel the influences of the planets as they come upon the mundane angles.

constructed in no arbitrary manner, but that it is derived from real principles of the utmost importance.

It is these which it is our present intention to study. Much has been written about them; much more will be written, and, as time goes on, man will wonder more and more profoundly at the knowledge which his early ancestors possessed and delineated for the perpetual instruction of humanity. When the last word has been said about the Zodiac the last mystery that confronts mankind will have been solved.

We must begin with the principle of Polarity, by which we divide the signs into positive and negative, or masculine and feminine, alternately.

This principle is, of course, familiar to all students of occult science, although it seems absurd that the clear statement of so very obvious a law should have to be sought for in what is called occult, or hidden.

There can be few systems of ancient thought in which it is not prominent, but perhaps in none is it so fundamental as in Taoism, under the names of Yang and Yin. Those who wish to study it in terms of human psychology cannot do better than turn to C. G. Jung's commentary upon the Taoist scripture *The Secret of the Golden Flower*. Yet in such matters one ought not to rely too much upon reading; they should be made the objects of personal meditation and reflection.

"*The Monad is extended, and begetteth the Two*," says the Chaldean Oracle, in which the Second Principle is regarded as Power—the power by which the One causes Itself to become manifest.

I have often felt, for example, "that there is some Mars about", and, on referring to the ephemeris, have found him on an angle. This sensitivity is, of course, most pronounced when the planet in question is active by transit or direction in the observer's horoscope.

Astrologically the positive signs are related, by analogy, to the Manifest, and the negative to the Unmanifest, the Sun being the ruling principle of the former and the Moon of the latter. But Astrology can scarcely place one before the other, either in dignity or in sequence. It begins, so far as our written doctrine is concerned, with a dualism, and if we seek, in astrology, the ONE that is behind the TWO, we must use some such symbol as the point within the zodiacal circle. Our venerable Chaldean predecessors, as we are told, had no name for that ONE, nor ever mentioned It. The mind cannot rest content with a duality; it must, even if in reverential silence, turn to the Unity behind all things. But this ONE is not so much the Unmanifest as that which is beyond all conceptions of manifestation. It does not enter into practical astrology at all, for this begins with the Zodiac and its division into the two polarities.

The dichotomy which gives us masculine and feminine signs operates a second time, and the masculine fall into two groups, and the feminine into two more. These four are named after the four medieval elements. Fire and air are masculine, and earth and water are feminine.

But, besides this, we may with perfect correctness divide the four elements by placing air and earth together, and, on the other side, fire and water. The actuality of this division may be seen by reference to the rulers. Mercury, Venus, and Saturn rule one airy and earthy sign apiece, and similarly the Sun–Moon, Mars, and Jupiter rule one fiery and one watery sign each. The practical value of this division lies in the connection of fire–water with the emotions, and air–earth with the mind.

These two divisions resemble a classing of the first four numerals as 1–2 and 3–4, and as 1–3 and 2–4.

We may present these bisections diagrammatically, thus:

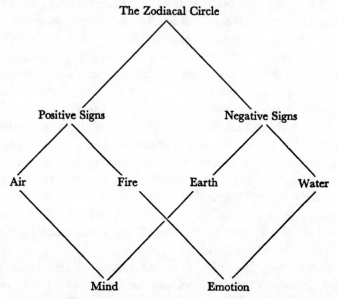

The Zodiacal Circle

Positive Signs　　　　　Negative Signs

Air　　　Fire　　　Earth　　　Water

Mind　　　Emotion

It will be seen that there is no technical term for air–earth and fire–water as classes, such as there is for fire–air (positive) and earth–water (negative). But it is open to question whether the former division is not equally important.

The principle of positivity is that which is outgoing, active, and manifest, while that of negativity is indrawn, passive, and unmanifest.[1] But, in the customary sense in which the

[1] We shall not err if we state that there is an analogy between the astrological polarities and the twin principles of Spirit and Matter. These we may conceive as being under exactly opposite laws, symbolised in Astrology by another duality, that of benefic and malefic planets, considered as two classes. So far as matter is concerned, the malefics rule it, and all material things from Sun, Moon, and Stars to the pettiest monument of human pride must ultimately go into dissolution and nothingness. Viewed from this point, our efforts to maintain health are a

word is used, the negative signs are often very active. That activity, however, is interior and private rather than external and public. Contrast the open liberality of Sagittary with the secret beneficences of Pisces.

The differences between air–earth and fire–water relate to the parts of man's nature which they severally affect, as indicated in the above diagram.

Before leaving the discussion of polarity it is well to remind the reader that the first half of the Zodiac and the first six houses of the mundane figure are of the negative character. So, too, contrasted with the eastern side of the figure, are the western quadrants. Thus the fourth, fifth, and sixth houses are the most latent part of the map.

The four elements, which, of course, have no relation to the numerous elements of modern chemistry, are called by astrologers the four Triplicities, because each contains three signs and operates in a threefold manner. It is this triple aspect of the four elements that gives rise to the twelve signs.

---

losing battle, fought desperately in order to delay the evil day of physical death. Wealth is a mere means to prolong the same fight against indigence and the final victory of natural forces, and Success is a momentary triumph that must end in the debility and helplessness of old age. Spirit is under the law of self-perpetuation and self-progression. In man, and, we are told, in man alone, placed as the Pymander says "in the blessed station of the middle", these two principles contend, a fact symbolised by the square aspect, which falls in signs of diverse polarity. Man can turn either way, and either build himself trines in positive signs or in negative, the former favouring spiritual powers, the latter material ones. As to how far man can actually acquire prepotency over matter, by developing his spiritual nature, time must show. It is certain that all great philosophers have attained to an inner indifference to physical limitations, but this is not the same as to vanquish them. Astrology begins, as we said, with polarity, and ordinary astrology ends when man transcends the Zodiac by gathering into himself the real values of all the signs.

The triadic principle has been known from times of unknown antiquity, and is of the utmost value. Indeed, it
would be hard to find any sentence fraught with deeper
meaning and yet of more transparent simplicity than the
Chaldean Oracle, which says, "*In every world shineth a Triad,
of which One is the ruling principle.*"

In Astrology the triadic principle produces what are known
as the three Quadruplicities, because each comprises four
signs. A less cumbrous and more expressive term is *Mode of
Action*, using the word mode like the Latin *modus* or English
mood, in its grammatical sense, as a method of expression.
The three modes are, of course, known traditionally as the
cardinal, the fixed, and the common or mutable. We may
also call them dynamic, static, and harmonious or ideal.
They are related in human psychology to the conative aspect
of consciousness, which desires to do, the pleasure–pain
aspect, which moves us to seek the pleasant and avoid the
noxious, and the cognitive or thought-aspect. A very common comparison is made to the three Hindu gunas, which are
rajas, tamas, and *sattva*, but astrologers, as such, do not
commonly regard the mutable signs as having the perfection,
relatively to the others, which the Gita ascribes to *sattva*.

However, it is true that the common signs have in them a
certain possibility of completeness that is denied to the others.

For the Triad arises in this way: the ONE produces the
TWO, and then the Two become the THREE by the appearance of a third factor, which is called common because it
contains something of each parent, being therefore a common
meeting-place or point of reconciliation between these two,
who otherwise would be entirely opposed.[1]

In a certain sense we may call the Fixed Mode the father,

[1] See Plato's *Timaeus*, 31 c.

the Cardinal the mother, and the Common the child, and one cannot avoid seeing how true this analogy is in ordinary life when the children often provide the common ground whereon the parents can meet and a link between them.

In Astrology we are used to regarding Venus as the great conciliator, and she, it may be objected, is a ruler of cardinal and fixed signs. But (and this must be stressed) in what, for lack of a better term, we must call esoteric astrology, it is the exaltation rulership which is most illuminating, if not always, at any rate frequently. In this light we see Venus as ruler over the mutable sign Pisces, and thus the planet of harmony is intimately connected with the mode of the same nature.[1]

The Modes may also be explained in terms of motion, the cardinal being movement, the fixed non-movement, and the common an alternation of movement and non-movement. Or we may call them linear, circular, and vibratory motion. Many analogies occur to the mind, and although different, they are not mutually contradictory. Mystically the modes are the abiding, proceeding, and returning aspects of Deity, and, again, they are the going forth of the soul from God, the abiding of the soul in God through the Spirit, and the return of the soul to conscious union.

In occult science the primal Triad is, of course, that of the three Logoi, which are commonly called those of Love, Wisdom, and Power. How shall we relate these to the three Modes?

[1] It may be objected that there is nothing especially harmonising about Gemini, Virgo, or Sagittary, all three of which are often given to argumentation and hair-splitting. But these disputations are directed towards the ultimate integration of thought. Venus tends to see resemblances and ignore differences. The mutable see differences and set actively to work to reconcile them.

Love is certainly an emotional state, and may be attributed to the fixed mode, and in particular to the Sun and Leo, although we have its negative aspect in the Moon and Cancer, watchful, forethoughtful, and providential.

Wisdom is not inappropriate to the Moon and Cancer, but, as a whole, the cardinal mode hardly seems to suggest this virtue. The "shrewdness" and "prudence" of Cancer often mentioned in text-books, may be mundane reflections of Divine Wisdom. But surely Love would not be an attribute lacking from the Great Mother.

Again, most astrologers would say that *Power* should be attributed to the Sun and Leo.

The Sun and Moon are, of course, astrologically two poles of one principle, which, writing as an astrologer, I would call *Power*, or, more abstractly, simple Being. Love to us is rather a specialised influence transmitted by Venus—Power modified and tempered, as it were, to our needs, the might of the Sun and the loving-kindness of the Moon.

Wisdom would be given by an astrologer to the Common Cross, and in particular to Sagittarius.

As astrologers we cannot really recognise a true trinity of three equal Principles. We can only recognise the two poles of one principle—the cardinal-fixed modes—and a third derivative principle.

The Sun–Moon is the symbol of the first, with Venus, Mars, and Saturn as specialised aspects, each ruling one cardinal and one fixed sign.

Psychologically these show that action (cardinal cross) is desire (fixed cross) in operation. There is a perpetual interplay between them. Desire drives to action and the results of action kindle fresh desires.

The Common Cross, possessing two rulers which are lords

only of common signs and none other, stands apart, as Mind should stand apart from desire.

Most astrologers, I suppose, would place Wisdom under Jupiter, or, if we have to place it under a mode, then they would select the Common, agreeing with the Chaldeans, as we shall see. In the ordinary sense of the word Power would never be attributed by an astrologer to the common signs. It is true that "Knowledge gives Power", but it is not itself Power. The typical mutable man, as we know him astrologically, often possesses the key to power and yet does not use it, frequently allowing others to reap the material results of his labours.

In the Chaldean system (to which reference is appropriate, since the Chaldeans appear to have received and cherished more than any others the astrological aspects of the Arcane Tradition) the third principle of the Primal Triad was Mind, the first being the Father, and the second Power. These may easily be related to the first three signs, of which Aries is the exaltation of the Sun and Taurus of the Moon. The Chaldeans also taught that each of the three had an abiding, proceeding, and returning aspect. Following this conception, we may relate Aries to the Father, and may then say that Cancer is its abiding aspect, Libra its proceeding, and Capricorn its returning. Similarly with Taurus, Leo being the abiding, Scorpio the proceeding, and Aquarius the returning. Gemini is then the third Logos, Mind, and has its abiding aspect in Virgo, the unadventurous, its proceeding in Sagittarius the voyager and wanderer, and its returning in Pisces.

It will be well now to consider how astrologers use these several classifications.

Briefly, we may say that the three Modes, of whose philosophic value we have already written something, have a

B

definite and common use in practical astrology in reference to
rapidity of action, or otherwise. The Moon in a cardinal
sign, we say, means quick results and an early *dénouement*. But
if it is a fixed sign, then the outcome of the affair under consideration may be long delayed, while the mutable signs show
change and uncertainty. In character the cardinal signs
show the man who is prompt in action—*rebus natus agendis*.
This type is the doer and the one who dares. The fixed man
is stable, authoritative, and apt at arrangement and ordering.
The common type is mentally active, inquisitive, adaptable,
and a learner and teacher.

The Modes do not seem to affect our deeper nature, but
rather concern the pitch, so to speak, of the instrument.

The positive–negative division is very fundamental, and
corresponds to some extent to the extrovert and introvert
classes of modern psychology, the man who lives in action
and performance, looking outward and forward, and he
whose inner life is rich, but whose gaze is directed rather
towards the past, originating little.

The positive signs tend always to make changes, the
negative take things as they are.

The Triplicities also lie at the very root of our natures. Fire
is the impulse towards self-assertion, and water the instinct of
self-preservation and the impulse to protect, the object of its
solicitude becoming larger as the character expands. Air is,
when fully active, the intellect, and, combined with water,
corresponds to Imagination. Earth is related to the concrete
mind, that which knows *what* a thing is, but cannot say why
it is, or what its significance is.

Fire may be related to Religion, Earth to Natural Science,
Air to Philosophy, and Water to Art. But each of these four
may be again subdivided. Thus, Semitic religion, with its

specially theocentric tendency and its high development of the moral aspect, is peculiarly connected with fire. Chinese religious thought, which is humanistic and anthropocentric, has a relation to air. Aryan religion, which is mainly a worship of natural forces, is earthy. The Negro cults, which are mostly necromantic and are closely akin to modern spiritism, are of water.

Throughout all things run the same chains of correspondence, from their source in the Divine Ideas downward. The astrological rules are valid because they reflect the action of these Ideas and tell of a Cosmos which moves in unison, singing, as it were, in concord. It is evident, from the study of horary astrology, that our very thoughts often "make one accord with the mundane circulation", as Plotinus says, and a very large part of our character—all, in fact, that we denote by the word temperament—is found to correspond with our nativities.

Thus it is that Astrology has profound psychological value.

Further, our bodies are equally or even more affected by the celestial bodies, and so our physical characteristics are shown astrologically and give rise to types which are seen to correspond to the divisions we have mentioned.

In a word, every kind of life may be classed astrologically; and although we must allow to the soul freedom of choice, within certain limits, yet it is undeniable that, at least in the generality of cases, the nature of its choice will not be at variance with the nativity, and, whatever its *choice*, its *freedom of action* will most assuredly be circumscribed by its horoscope of birth. Only by knowledge and unceasing effort do we attain to some sort of volitional freedom; our tools are shown in our birth-maps, and we can do little to change them. But we may select which we will use, we may improve in the use of them, we may even sharpen them and keep them keen and clean, and we may employ them on work, within limits, of our own selection.

Water, we may say, is related to the occult or mystical point of view. These terms have diverse usages; but occult means hidden, and the mystical is properly that concerning which we close our lips in veneration. Water pertains to that which is latent rather than obvious, and sacred rather than profane. It has special relation to the Secret Tradition, which has been made to some extent public since the discovery of Neptune. It holds the keys to the Mysteries of Birth, Death, and Resurrection; the past, present, and future of the soul of humanity and of the individual. All the signs are in some sense mysteries, and each contains symbolically something which may be called an initiation; but the three watery signs are the three great astrological Arcana.

This small book is written in the main from a mystical point of view; it is designed to interest those whose thoughts trend in that direction. Sympathy with a certain point of view is taken for granted: those who adopt other attitudes of mind will seek their inspiration elsewhere. What has been written in this section may be of some use to any astrologer, except indeed the most superficial and empiric, but in succeeding sections I shall write for a limited circle, to whom the secrets of the Watery Triad are not mere matters of fantasy.

The task of interpreting the zodiacal script has been attempted by many writers, each approaching the work from his own standpoint. The contents of the Circle of Zodiacal Wisdom are inexhaustible, and present all-various aspects of the integrity of Truth.

II

THE ZODIAC AND THE UNFOLDMENT OF
THE SOUL

I BELIEVE, and many believe with me, that the Zodiac por-
trays the pathway of the soul of man and of humanity.

On the other hand, there are, at the present time, very
many more who either do not believe in any soul at all, either
of individual or of race, or who are entirely agnostic as to its
nature, origin, and destiny.

But unless man, as an individual, possessed a principle of
unity, he could neither think nor act coherently.

Further, it is evident upon consideration that the soul is a
simple substance, and, as such, cannot suffer the dissolution
which we call death and which must befall all compound
things, but only them.

Again, since man possesses intelligence, it stands to reason
that his Creator must possess the same attribute, for otherwise whence could human intelligence have come? And since
the lesser cannot create the greater, Divine Intelligence must
necessarily transcend the human.

But to create without purpose would be contrary to sense,
and therefore it cannot be supposed that man has been thus
created.

Man has a purpose and that this is an eternal purpose we
see, analogically, in the circular Zodiac, which has no real

beginning or end, when viewed as a whole and not as so many signs.

For our present purpose let us regard the Zodiac as comprising four sections, each of three successive signs. These sections I shall call, naming them in their sequence from Aries, the Fontal Triad, the Natural Triad, the Human Triad, and the Superhuman Triad.

The Fontal Triad
Aries—Taurus—Gemini

The first three signs have several peculiarities in common, when viewed from the standpoint of ordinary astrology. There is something crude and indifferentiate about them. Aries represents rude energy, such as we associate with the cave-man or vigorous and powerful savage. Taurus recalls the primeval also; the sign is near to Mother Earth, and carries the mind back to the shepherd and herdsman. Gemini is by no means so unsophisticated, yet there is the same lack of complexity about it. It is intellect, pure and simple, neither good nor evil, kind nor unkind, honest nor dishonest, youthful and fresh, delighting in the exercise of its powers and as yet hardly using them for any specialised purpose. The mind flashes hither and thither, like a child playing with a mirror in the sun and throwing the beam of light into dark corners. There is a naïve egotism about all three. Aries is self-opinionated, Taurus stubbornly self-willed, and Gemini often conceited.

From the standpoint of morality one must admit that all three stand rather low.[1]

---

[1] That is to say, from a purely empirical standpoint. Statistics show that these signs are more frequently tenanted by planets in criminal horoscopes than the law of averages would lead us to expect. See chapter on The Violent Criminal in the writer's *Some Principles of Horoscopic Delineation*.

Yet Aries, Taurus, and Gemini stand for the three Logoi; they are the signs of the Sun, Moon, and Mercury.[1]

This apparent anomaly is due to the fact that we as human beings are studying these principles from below. When we compile statistics about the three first signs we are not dealing with the Logoi; far from it—we are engaged upon their reflections in the lower worlds. From *our* point of view, Aries, Taurus, and Gemini are crude and unrefined forces, near to the primitive and not yet adapted to the uses of mankind, which, as a whole, has passed to a later stage of development. To us the first triad is a reservoir of forces which change in the course of passing onward.

Each of these three belongs to one of the three Modes and represents the ideal combination, as it were, of mode and triplicity. Thus fire is truest to type when operating in the cardinal mode, which is Aries; earth is most earthy in the fixed mode, which is Taurus; and air is seen at its purest in the common mode, which is Gemini.

As the Chaldean Oracles say, each of these three monadic principles, themselves derived from One, generates a triad to which it is itself as the One is to the Primal Three. Thus:

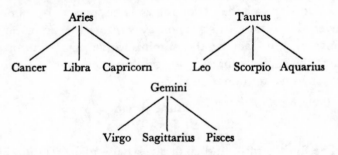

---

[1] Taking the exaltion-rulerships for the first two. In Gemini, of course, nothing is, so far as we know, exalted.

Thus each Mode flows through the four elements, and each element operates in terms of each Mode.

The process of unfoldment passes successively through the twelve signs, beginning with the Triad which I have called Fontal.

Life, as it were, is kindled in Aries, accumulates power in Taurus, and then flows freely into the common sign Gemini, where we may suggest that the Divine Ideas take distinctive shape and become the differentiated intellectual Archetypes of all that comes into existence in the objective worlds. No sign is more apt than Gemini to detect differences and appreciate the distinctive values and characters of separate things.

The three Principles belong properly to the Subjective World and have only a distant relation to human life as we know it, although that connection is fundamental. The rest of the Zodiac is a gradual development of these three in terms of Nature and Man. At least, it is in terms of the two that we can best study their unfolding. But we must not preclude the possibility of the existence of beings, zodiacally ordered, who are neither human nor parts of the world of Nature. The belief in the Celestial Hierarchies is supported by almost universal tradition, and is in no way contrary to reason. Such beings may in fact be the administrative powers through which the zodiacal forces work, and may for aught we know be responsive to human prayer.

The Natural Triad
Cancer—Leo—Virgo

The fourth, fifth, and sixth signs have plain relationship to the world of Nature. The first is symbolised by an aquatic or amphibious animal; the second, by the king of beasts, and the third, though human, holds a sheaf of corn, emblematic of the vegetable kingdom.

Cancer has relation to Taurus, since the Moon is exalted therein; and, if we begin with the Sun and Moon, and then count outwards, Mercury corresponds to Gemini and Venus to Cancer.[1]

In Cancer we see the progeny of Taurus, the Great Mother, the myriad archetypal Ideas brought down through the Intellect of Gemini into the seething Ocean of Generation. Cancer is Form, but, at this stage, the Forms are very fluidic; they are destined to become concrete and particular in Capricornus. Manifestation is still young, and Cancer is a shrinking, retiring sign, though interiorly intensely active. It comes before the public, but half unwillingly. So we may conceive the Forms as highly sensitive and yet teeming in occult activity.

The lack of rude energy in Cancer is shown by the square from it to Aries—the first square, and truly the origin of evil, as we call it. Here the soul for the first time becomes conscious of limitation. Pain is not yet present, for self-consciousness has not arrived.

We may briefly consider the problem of Pain, to which indeed we shall recur.

In the first Triad evil was not possible, for the Three were complete and the possibility of conflict which is inherent in the different polarities of Aries and Taurus was resolved by

---

[1] This method of relating planet and sign is not without value. In effect, it relates each planet to the sign on the mid-heaven when its own sign rises. Thus, when Virgo rises, Gemini culminates; when Libra rises, Cancer culminates, and so forth. This, however, gives the Sun to Taurus and the Moon to Aries, reversing the customary exaltations. But the Sun and Moon are, philosophically, two aspects of one Principle.

the presence of Gemini, which, as a common sign, harmonised them. But when a fourth sign comes into the field a fresh step is taken; there is that which is exterior to the Primal Harmony. Four cannot be derived from three. Each fourth sign is of the Watery Triplicity and is symbolic of a temporary submersion and dissolution. In Cancer the Forms are in intimate and harmonious relationship to Taurus, but they are broken off by the square from Aries and experience a sense of feebleness and inadequacy. Moreover, every square denotes in one sense a thwarting or checking of force, producing repression prior to a sudden release of energy in fresh directions.

The exaltation of Jupiter in Cancer seems to show the boundless prolificacy of this world.

Cancer, again, is specially the sign of the Soul, both of Man and of Nature; the brooding oversoul which is the living principle behind the manifest Cosmos, cherishing and nourishing it.

Leo receives the trine of Aries, and here the Forms are instantly replenished with energy. The Lives become objective and vital; they no longer abide in the Womb of Cancer, but go forth in physical life.

Virgo gives perfect bodily form, being, as we know, the sign of that physical perfection which is seen in Nature. It represents the Edenic or Golden Age. It is a sign of perfection, intolerant of inordination. It is of the ideal or common mode, with no strong aspect to Aries, and therefore inclined, as we see in ordinary life, to maintain a state of happy innocence, busied with simple things. The trine of Taurus shows how the Great Mother, through the Cancerian Oversoul, fosters her children. The square to Gemini shows that intelligence is present, but that self-consciousness has still to come. The animal world lives close to the great Heart of Leo, in a condition of natural integrality.

It is not without interest that Virgo is still the sign of Orchards and Gardens.

The Human Triad
Libra—Scorpio—Sagittary

Libra, at one time united (according to legend) in one sign with Virgo and Scorpio, is the sign of man in his early innocence, already endowed with self-consciousness through the Gemini trine, the opposition to Aries showing that he has developed this attribute, and with it, the possibility of separation from his Father. He can, indeed, recognise the difference between himself and others, self and not-self. The square from Cancer shows the beginning of a fresh cycle and the break away from the Oversoul, which guides the lives of animals through their natural instincts.

Self-conscious thought is really born of the square between Gemini and Virgo—it is at this point that the Elohim, the Creator Spirits before the Throne of the Geminian Third Logos, say, "Let Us make man in Our Image." The tasting of the apple, in the story of Genesis, seems to refer to Libra, for Venus rules apples, and it was to Venus that Paris awarded an apple in the famous myth. The Fall seems to have reference to the exaltation of Saturn in Libra, and is, in astrological parlance, an Opposition—the opposition which divides self-conscious man from his Father Sun in Aries. The Sun, of course, has its "fall" in Libra.

There is a certain well-known weakness and dependence about Libra, not unlike that of Cancer, and similarly the result of a new birth into unfamiliar conditions. Man has now passed out of the walled and angel-guarded Eden, and has become the independent Thinker. His mind may, through the trine of Gemini, become illuminated at once by the Divine Intellections of Gemini, and it is possible that some may pass to their goal without suffering the Ordeal of Scorpio.

But the generality feel in Libra the square of Cancer and yearn instinctively for the protection of the Great Mother which they have now lost. They are forsaken, or, as it seems to them, betrayed, by a Woman, and thus go into the "far country" of alienation from Divinity, failing to actualise the ideal of freedom in conformity with God.

We are again confronted with a Mystery in the second watery sign Scorpio. This is the Mystery of Death, not only our ordinary death, but the death which is physical life.

Scorpio, of all the signs, has no good aspect to the Fontal Triad. It is in opposition to Taurus and has the quincunx, which is in effect a weak opposition, to Aries and Gemini. Hence it is termed the "accursed" sign. It is in square to Leo, the sign of physical life, and so it is physical death. The Genesis curses are all Scorpionic. Death, sexual shame, painful parturition, toil, sweat, thorns, and thistles are all reminiscent not of Saturn but of Mars. We have the murder of Abel and the Flood, which fittingly ended this epoch.

·   ·   ·   ·   ·

Mankind in Scorpio is in darkness, alienation, and rebellion. He cannot die, except in a physical sense, because of the trine aspect from Cancer. Although the square of Leo plunges him into the deep waters yet he suffers death only as regards the positive or solar part of him.

The nadir-point in his descent is the dividing line or cusp between Libra and Scorpio, opposing the cusp between

Aries and Taurus. But even here the gulf may be spanned, if, recalling the memory of his divine origin, he cries *de profundis* unto God and constructs by his aspirations a bridge of salvation across the abyss. He has died as physical man in the Third Triad, but the Zodiac is not yet ended, and there is space left for his resurrection as that which is more than man.

But man, self-conscious but not yet master of his new-born powers, usually falls a victim to the impulse to fight violently for his personal advantage and to maintain his self-hood in a world of contending entities of whom, as possible antagonists, he is now acutely conscious. He may carry his new independence to the extremes of separation not only from other souls, but from his Source. Hence Scorpio is a battlefield, whereon all the possibilities of sensation are explored.

Sometimes he turns abruptly from his revels and moral abandon, and becomes "converted". When this happens it represents a leap forward from Scorpio to Pisces, usually by way of the asceticism of the sextile sign, Capricornus. More often the savage gradually tires of his savagery, which ends in death and dissolution so far as the objects of its desires are concerned. Something better must be found, and the soul launches its Argo to seek the Golden Fleece—that is, its father Aries.

Sagittarius is in trine to Aries, but in opposition to Gemini, while Taurus is merely in quincunx—appropriately, since a new venture must be begun and the influence of the great negative sign would always be against fresh enterprise, such as, in this sign, is typified by the Centaur with his full-drawn bow. Aries now calls to his Son from afar, calls to him in the Egypt of Scorpio. We have come to the last fiery sign, pure

Emotion, which may be called Aspiration. Sagittary represents the perfect man at the end of the Third Triad, wherein spirit strives with man, for that he also is flesh, that is, man is still corporeal and at work in the corporeal world, and the spirit urges him on and upward.

The worst of mankind are still today in the world of Scorpio, the malignant and impure. Many good men are in the same world, the men of stubborn courage. Many of the best of men are still in Sagittarius, those of real enlightenment and benevolence.

It is appropriate that this sign should be ruled by Jupiter, the Liberator and Preserver, the God to whom the vast majority of mankind should direct their prayers today for breadth of outlook and wideness of sympathy. The sign has also affinity with Neptune, and is a foretaste of the final liberation of Pisces. Scorpio is under Mars and perhaps Uranus, the two most violent planets, self-willed, dominating, and haughty, but possessing great intensity of will and purpose.[1] Their extreme individualism is to be expected in view of the condition that Scorpio represents. Sagittarius, emerging joyfully from Satanic desperation, is characterised by profusion, disregard of limitation, and a candour and generosity which clearly show the dawning of larger conceptions. The native of the sign tends to disregard time and space, being exoterically notorious for his unpunctuality and general lack of precision. His vitality is immense ($\ꭗ$ $\triangle$ Ω), but in matters of form he is weak and careless ($\ꭗ$ $\square$ m). The intellect is alert and energetic, but exaggerative ($\ꭗ$ $\mathcal{S}$ II), and in its new found liberty it is impatient and prone to try to take the Kingdom by storm.

[1] Since this was written Pluto has also come into our ken, with a probable relation to Scorpio.

The square between it and Virgo indicates that there has arisen a consciousness of the breach that has definitely come between man and brute, as the centaur-symbol also denotes. Man must leave the animal kingdom.

But when the soul, impelled by the inherent energy and daring of fire, rushes forward, it meets a rigid barrier to its high-flown aspirations.

The Superhuman Triad
Capricorn—Aquarius—Pisces

Capricorn is doubly linked with the material world, for it is the sign of Saturn and the exaltation of Mars, lords of the physical and astral planes.

Man must not seek to pass beyond these realms until he has subjected them, and in Capricorn, the great organising and ruling sign, this must be done. To despise and reject earth is not difficult, seeing how unpleasant our terrestrial lives frequently are. Many earnest souls take this course, and many who are simply indolent or inefficient.

The perfection of Virginian nature must now receive its complement in a perfect human order, manifest in the objective world. Even man's corporeal body must be mastered and made to serve his will.

The square from Libra seems to indicate the struggle which the soul here encounters. She is definitely on the upward path, as the climbing Goat indicates, but her efforts must be unceasing. Too often the myth of Sisyphus is the story of the experiences of this sign; but the end is certain. The square from Libra insists on complete realisation and there can be no permanent halt.

Sorrow, in some form, seems part of the heritage of the negative signs. Taurus must grieve over the birth-pangs of Cancer. Virgo, madonna-like, must see the agony of its children, cast out from its bosom. Scorpio is the sorrow of the battlefield, whereon all the adverse forces seem to gather together, like the waters of the Red Sea, to menace the advance of the soul. Capricorn is the ordeal of patient labour, by which the lessons of Matter are vanquished one by one. We have reached the opposition of Cancer, and the formal side of manifestation is complete. Ten is the number of Completion, and Capricorn is the tenth sign.

We have worked through the Zodiac as it was when Saturn was the limit of our outlook. Man, as seen from below, is now perfect and complete. Having obtained the mastery of matter he must turn to other and more occult tasks. May we surmise that Aquarius means the conscious and complete reconciliation of the Two Realms, that of Matter and that of Spirit, in Man, who stands at the meeting-point of each? Uranus has undoubtedly some special relation to Aquarius, and Uranus is, I consider, the great intermediary between the Above and the Below, and hence the Awakener and the Initiator. Uranus, too, is said to be a planet of the ether, and this again has significance, for the study of etheric phenomena leads us to understand the true nature of matter, even if it does not bring us to the noumenal.

In Pisces, it seems, Man departs from the physical realms; it is the sign of self-denial, of seclusion, and withdrawal. It is of interest to consider what the real difference is between the limitation of Saturn and that of Pisces. The latter is said to rule imprisonment, and yet this seems strange in a sign that is in part Jovian; the whole meaning of Pisces seems rather to be looseness, relaxation, dissolution, and nebulosity—states which, in terms of character, mean irresponsible carelessness, all that is easy-going, free-and-easy, and do-as-you-please.

It is clear that these tendencies often end in the workhouse, asylum, or jail, but I find it hard to believe that any kind of compulsory detention is Piscean; it is the *seclusion* which belongs to that sign; the stone walls and iron bars are surely Saturnian. Pisces, the sign of redemption, may hand over those whom its waters cannot cleanse to the stern ringed planet, but its own bonds are far more subtle than physical imprisonment.

Pisces may in fact be the sign of *Nunc Dimittis*, when the soldier is discharged from arduous duties and returns to his own home. In any case it is certainly a sign in which the Soul is by no means at home in matter, and often seeks to evade the duties of an unaccustomed condition, seeking too frequently to revive the exalted states of the Spiritual Country by recourse to drugs and stimulants. Perhaps its truest function is that of an interpreter of spiritual things to human beings, a difficult task indeed, and one that necessitates a sensitive body as well as a pure soul. How can we expect the Piscean to be happy, if its duty is to remember what is Yonder whilst it is incarcerated Here? *Nessun maggior dolore!*

Symbolically Pisces is the state of the Blessed—the purified Souls in Elysium, liberated for a time from the bondage of Hyle; ultimately it is the symbol of the final freedom and attainment; in the most limited sense it is just Sleep, which is our daily rest. All Neptunian souls show the same stirrings of desire for this Elysian life. It may be a mere fretfulness or petulance, the reason and meaning of which neither the child of ocean nor his friends can divine; it may be the agonised yearning of the blind; it may move beneath the calm assurance of the sage, or it may take expression in lines such as those of Shelley:

c

"The One remains, the many change and pass;
Heaven's light for ever shines, Earth's shadows fly;
Life, like a dome of many-coloured glass,
Stains the white radiance of Eternity,
Until Death tramples it to fragments."

In any case we shall all arrive at the true Home of Souls. It may be so long before this happens as to be almost an eternity, or it may be, for each one of us, very soon. Those who have tasted, if but momentarily, the Neptunian state of consciousness are not likely again to overvalue earthly attractions or to recommend tarrying by the roadside.

III

THE SIGNS AND PLANETS AS COSMIC IDEALS

EACH sign may be considered as a Cosmic Principle or Ideal and each of these gives rise to a characteristic human virtue, although it is not always easy to find an appropriate term for them. Corresponding to each Ideal there is a typical human delusion or heresy, giving rise to characteristic human faults, defects, or shortcomings.

The ensuing are written in the spirit of suggestion and as a framework for individual study.

Aries is the principle of Cosmic Individuality, which is the truth that everything of which we can speak or even think is a unity and possesses the rights of a unity. This, in a sense, may also be called Cosmic Strength. It gives rise to the virtue of Courage, and as its counterpart it has the delusion of egotism, or the belief that the rights of the individual are his only concern, the "struggle for existence" being deemed a permanent fact, beyond which it is not necessary to look. This produces such faults as arrogance.

Taurus is the principle of Cosmic Stability or Certitude. In the spiritual world there is complete certainty and finality, but in mundane existence truth is often relative and partial. The virtue of Stability is usually called Reliability. The delusion that corresponds is staticism—the belief that things are best as they are, and that progress, intellectual or material, is unnecessary and undesirable. The fault of the sign is perhaps best named rigidity, with such secondary tendencies as stubbornness and tyranny.

Gemini is Cosmic Distinctiveness, or the truth that everything has its distinct use and purpose, down to the smallest particular. This is evinced in the Geminian love of detail, and it gives rise to the virtue of Knowledge of Differences, by which the natives of the sign owe their peculiar powers of appreciating inter-relationships and the bearings that parts have to one another and to the whole. The corresponding delusion is that of separateness, or the belief that parts are not only distinct but separate, whence arises the fault of hardness.

Cancer is the principle of Cosmic Protection or Providence. From this comes the virtue of Solicitude, or Care for Others. The delusion is favouritism, or belief that we should care for our own group or family, but that those beyond that pale are of no account. Partiality and Partisanship are similar errancies. Where there is a failure to understand this principle we get distrust and foreboding, producing such faults as superstition—the turning to ridiculous omens, mascots and similar absurdities, for that protection which should be sought from Divine Providence.

Leo is the principle of Cosmic Splendour. There is a natural and inherent magnificence in real greatness, which those who possess an element of greatness in themselves feel and respect. The human virtue is Magnanimity. The delusion is pretence, or the belief that outward show constitutes real grandeur; and this engenders such faults as ostentation, vainglory, and vulgar pretentiousness.

Virgo is the principle of Cosmic Perfection, or the truth that all things are now or will become perfect. This produces the virtue of Thoroughness or Perfectiveness. The delusion is that of minutism, or inordinate devotion to detail without due regard to the importance and significance of the whole. The consequent faults are lack of perspective and pettiness.

This sign seems also to correspond to the Cosmic Principle of Usefulness, of which the virtue is Practicality, the delusion Utilitarianism, and the faults lack of spiritual aspiration and appreciation.

Libra is the principle of Cosmic Reciprocity or Mutuality, by which all things have mutual relationships and reciprocal rights and obligations. This produces the virtues of fairness, co-operativeness, and helpfulness. The heresy is that of Parasitism, or the belief that it is natural for some to attach themselves to others and derive their support and even ideas and motives at second-hand. This naturally produces the fault of dependence and sycophancy.

Scorpio is the sign of the principle of Cosmic Purpose. All things possess purpose and are in a condition of being trained or shaped to that end. Hence we get the virtue of self-culture, since the preparation for man's purpose is largely in his own hands. The Scorpio native has a profound belief in self-training and self-discipline, and he is the most purposeful of all men. The delusion is that of Despotism, or the belief that the individual can override the Divine Order; and from this comes the fault of rebelliousness. Vindictiveness arises from the same heresy, for the despot, believing that there is no Divine Governance or justice, attempts to take the law into his own hands.

Sagittary is Cosmic Progress, or the truth that all things perpetually move to higher and higher conditions of physical, affectional, and intellectual unfoldment. Hence arise the virtues of progressiveness, hopefulness, and faith. The delusion that corresponds is restlessness, or the love of novelty for its own sake, with such faults as inconstancy, lack of perseverance, wastefulness, over-optimism, and prodigality.

To this sign we may also relate the principle of Cosmic Abundance, or the truth that there is potentially more than enough for all the needs of humanity. This, perverted, gives rise to prodigality, which tends to produce the last three of the above faults.

Capricorn is Cosmic Order and Justice, embodied in the truth that "As ye sow so shall ye reap." From this arises the virtue of respect for those worthy of respect and the faculty of appreciating the hierarchical ideal, by which the lesser always subserve the higher.

From this principle may come the delusion of formalism, or literalism, the belief that the form is greater than the spirit, the letter more important than the idea.

Materialism, as a heresy or delusion, probably comes under all three of the earthy signs, but most of all under Taurus.

Mediocritism, or the belief that the commonplace and usual are the best; that genius is dangerous, and that great men are best out of the way, belong perhaps to Virgo, but may arise from the excessive respect for Order which comes chiefly under the present sign.

Aquarius is the principle of Cosmic Solidarity, from which arises the virtue of brotherliness. The heresy of the sign is Sociolatry, or the belief that the individual should count as little or nothing compared with the community. Hence arises a lack of belief in that unique value which belongs inalienably to every soul, and a tendency to what may be called indistinctness of personality and personal aspiration.

Pisces is Cosmic Grace, or Forgiveness, from which comes

the virtue of charity. The delusion is that of irresponsibility, or the erroneous belief that we need not face the consequences of our actions and thoughts, and from this are generated such faults as shiftlessness, imprudence, and purposelessness.

It will be noticed that it is not always easy to differentiate as between the signs of the same Triplicity. Moreover, while the principles, being cosmic, are usually distinct and unitary, the delusions and faults, being ultimate reflections, are often confused and numerous. Even language shows this; there are words for almost every shade of shortcomings, but sometimes none at all for a universal principle.

In common life it is the animal spirits which give trouble in fire, the habits and moods in water, the lack of aspiration and breadth of interest in earth, and the lack of common sense and perspective in air.

The Planets

The intimate association between the Sun, Moon, and planets on one side and the Zodiac on the other justifies us in briefly considering the former in respect of the ideal principles which they reflect.

But we must beware of expecting exact correspondence, firstly because, as physical existences, it should not be expected that they will furnish exact reflections of ideal principles, and, secondly, because we have no certitude that our knowledge of the planets is complete. The medieval astrologers were able to rest, well satisfied with their security, on the Sun, Moon and Five Planets, and on these they constructed a complete and logical scheme of rulerships. But the discovery of Uranus and of Neptune, and, still later, of

Pluto has reduced this scheme to a very dubious condition, and has, furthermore, made astrologers chary of constructing any other in its place, since the possibility of further discoveries is ever with us. One would not like to venture a forecast as to how far the rigid rulerships in use today will be recognised in the astrology of coming generations.

A general clue to the course of human evolution, as a race and individually, is given by the Exaltations.

Thus we take the Sun as the primal source of our existence. He is exalted in a sign of Mars, animal or passional man. Mars is exalted in a sign of Saturn, the lesser malefic in the sign of the greater. Thus man is first animal, and then self-conscious.

Saturn is exalted in the sign of Venus, the lesser benefic and Venus, again, is exalted in the sign of the greater benefic, denoting man's upward path or return to the ideal condition.

Lastly, Jupiter is exalted in the sign of the Moon.

Mercury, who has no exaltation, accompanies the soul throughout, instructing and guiding it.

Uranus is lord of the Descent into matter, combining the qualities of Mars and Saturn, but endowed with a far wider perception than either of them. He is, as it were, stationed in the material world, but he has a vision of both spheres.

Neptune is lord of the Return, combining Venus and Jupiter. His characteristic other-worldliness which often makes him, from our point of view, inefficient and maleficent, results from his peculiar function as one who leads away from the actual to the Real.

Since Neptune combines Venus and Jupiter it naturally follows that he is related to Pisces, the exaltation of the one and the sign of the other.

By analogy it would seem that Uranus would be related to

Capricorn, which is the exaltation of Mars and the sign of Saturn.

The above scheme, based on the exaltations, may also be set out in a diagram.

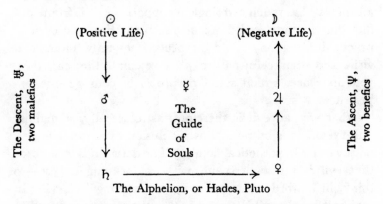

A consideration of the above will help us to understand what evil really is.

It is something which results from the contact of the soul with that which is not itself. Through this contact the soul learns to realise its potentialities and, above all, to understand its own nature, which it could not do, save by coming into contact and to some extent into conflict with something other than itself. Mars and Saturn, under the leadership of Uranus, usher it into these alien and uncongenial conditions, and so are called malefic influences. Venus, Jupiter, and Neptune remind it of its real nature and true home, singing songs to it, as it were, of its own country in a strange land. Mercury is its great educator, ruling the faculties by which it establishes contact with matter and with other souls, and comes to understand itself and them.

The malefic configurations, of which the Square is related

to Mars and the Opposition to Saturn, denote actual contacts with matter and material conditions in their uncongenial, or, as it seems, inimical aspect, providing incentives to self-unfoldment. The Greek aphorism that "War is the parent of all things" has much astrological support, for it is from conflict that strength and power are seen to arise, and even in practical horoscopy "bad" aspects frequently indicate a virile and resourceful nature; they resemble the scars on a veteran's face, which stand as proofs of courage and experience.

What we call evil is therefore, astrologically, something quite real. It is by no means a delusion of "mortal mind" or any other hypothetical faculty. The delusion is to suppose that evil is purposeless and without meaning or use—to think, in a word, that it *is* evil, and nothing but evil. In reality it is only evil in the sense that the whetstone is evil to the implement that is ground against it. But it is something distinctive. Mars, Saturn, and Uranus are actually different from Venus, Jupiter, and Neptune. Their virtues are practical and even severe. Fortitude, duty, and self-control are austere things compared with lovableness and munificence. It is to the life of the Soldier that the malefics call us, while the benefics lead us to the Gardens of the Gods, and sometimes, by themselves, spoil a person for actual life by taking the keen edge off the sword which the malefics forged and sharpened.

IV

THE ZODIAC AS A PATH TO THE GOOD

GOODNESS has special relation to our actions or conduct. This principle is now the subject of our inquiry in order that we may see how it operates in man and how it is depicted in the astrological symbology.

Being an ultimate reality, the Good cannot be defined, but all normal human beings understand something of the Ideal of Goodness.

From an occult standpoint we may say that Divine Providence perpetually flows into the Cosmos and into Man, but, by the misuse of his faculties, man may produce an apparent separation between himself and It, so that we have to study the perversions or distortions of Goodness, as well as its ideal expression. Indeed, in so far as Astrology is mainly concerned with ordinary humanity, it is the perversions which more usually meet us.

These perversions may be said to be due to one or other of the following causes: (*a*) excess, (*b*) deficiency, and (*c*) an incorrect use of providential forces, which, good in themselves, become maladjusted as the result of human action.

There is a correspondence between these three conditions and the cardinal, fixed, and common modes.

As an example we may take the principle that is related to

35

Mars. A man may have an excess of Martian activity, so that there is no rest or tranquillity in him; or he may have too little Mars, and be timid, weak, and indolent; or he may have, as we say, an afflicted Mars, and be quarrelsome or even brutal.

Technically speaking and in a general way, these three forms of perversion correspond to (a) the presence of many bodies in the signs of the planet in question or the prominence of the planet *mundo*, (b) the presence of many bodies in the signs of the opposite planet, or the prominence of that planet *mundo*, with a corresponding weakness of the planet in question, and (c) the presence of severe afflictions involving the planet in question by sign or by aspect to itself.

Thus, again using Mars as an example, a man with many bodies in Aries or Scorpio and with Mars on an angle, would have an excess. If he had no such conditions, but Venus was strong *mundo* and many bodies were in her signs, then the second condition would arise. If Mars were afflicted and severe afflictions fell in Aries or Scorpio, then the third condition would occur.

Yet, while any of these conditions may indicate lack of balance or even predispositions to undesirable tendencies, it would be wrong to assert that any of them *necessitate* bad conduct.

We will now study the astrological principles, using the system of classification set forth earlier.

Thus we begin with the division of the Signs into positive and negative categories.

The former has, as its correct expression, the power to advance, effect changes in the world, progress, and perform. This action may, of course, be excessive, defective, or inordinate, in which last case it becomes productive of the busybody, who ceaselessly inaugurates novelties, although there is no improvement in them, and undertakes new enterprises, although the old ones were not completed. In the worst cases the activities may be definitely directed to wrong and criminal ends.

The negative signs are the hidden side of life, in which the soul may be said to refresh itself in the penetralia of its own secret nature, as the body is refreshed in sleep. This type should possess a rich inner life, and often it performs many benefactions in secret. Privacy of action is congenial to this type; the perversion arises when the negative person seems to find no expression at all, and passes a dull, uneventful, and seemingly useless life, sometimes fettered by an intellectual conservatism, sometimes apparently inert and without desire or even passion.

Those whose studies have followed the lines of modern analytical psychology will be tempted to identify the positive signs with the Conscious and the negative with the Unconscious. And, in a broad sense, they would do rightly in this. But I am not so sure that the analogy can be carried strictly into practical work, so far as the mere presence of a majority of bodies in one or other of these two classes is considered. One strong contact, falling in a significant mundane position, may override the value of mere number.

The crimes of negative types tend to the sordid and disgusting, while those of the positives are more often bold and adventurous.

The too positive character is lacking in true intensity, constancy, and continuity; everything attracts but nothing holds.

The true negative seems to have no purpose and finds nothing attractive or provocative of action.

As regards training the former requires to realise the need

for depth of thought, patience and stability. He must be taught to submit to what he calls drudgery. He will often be impatient, careless, apt to jump to conclusions, and ready to take any hazard in order to avoid the trouble involved in adequate preparation. Similarly the emotional nature is likely to be superficial and fickle and the sense of responsibility small. As regards physical things, this class is apt to neglect and overwork the body, taking abundant exercise but little repose. They are often imprudent in matters of food and drink.

The negative type requires stimulation. The mind is usually either entirely practical, in the narrow sense of the term, or else it is dull, incurious, and pedestrian. It is well to elevate it to the contemplation of that which is abstract and spiritual, and so to purify its faculties; but, if this cannot be done (and in a sense it is not the *dharma* of the type), it should at least be energised in relation to practical affairs and made active in useful works, which will as a rule be constructive in the earth type, but remedial and alleviative in the water. The devotional nature, which is usually dormant in earth and is often given over to superstitious practices in the watery signs, has to be elevated and purified. The negative person is often interested in matters of physical health, even to the extent of unreasonable anxiety: this should be replaced by a sane interest in physical culture, as a worthy but not all-important pursuit.

Speaking in terms of the planets all inordinations require rectification by processes which may be related to Mercury, Jupiter, and Neptune, the planets of the Common Cross.

By the first, our natures are intellectualised, so that purely irrational, animal, and impulsive tendencies are corrected, and the various aspects of the psyche are harmoniously integrated.

By the second, the psyche is universalised by the unfoldment of ideal sympathies, so that the faculties are no longer occupied with the personal and partitive, but with the universal.

By the third, the entire being is lifted up to a mystical participation in the Divine.

These three processes may be traced even in conventional education, ordinary lessons being the Mercurial aspect; the inculcation of a sense of honour, of the "team-spirit", and of pride in one's house or school, being of the nature of Jupiter; and the religious instruction, nowadays as a rule probably often useless or even harmful to some natures in the manner in which it is presented, is Neptunian.

The three should, ideally, operate together, producing clarity of thought, healthy emotions, and purity of aspiration. "The lives of those who aspire as I do are all prayer," says Zanoni, and this is the highest aspect of fire and water.

Against these three may be placed certain obstructive tendencies.

In ordinary life these are mental inertia, selfishness, and lack of aspiration. These may be described astrologically as afflictions by Saturn of the three planets just mentioned. It is possible, however, to carry the process further, and tabulate typical inordinations corresponding, not only to all the planets and signs, but to their mutual inharmonious relationships.

But the above observations on the three mutable planets apply equally to all processes of mental alchemy by which our lesser natures are transmuted in the crucible of Mind.

It is necessary at this point to deal with the question, so often asked, as to whether we can, as it is expressed, *change our horoscopes*.

It is, of course, impossible to effect a radical or essential alteration, nor is it proper that we should aim at any such thing. The soul of every man, I believe, is unique, has a unique purpose, and a unique relationship to God. Astrologically speaking an Aries person is always an Aries, a Libran is a Libran, and so forth. This is assuredly true so far as this life is concerned, and what lies beyond cannot usefully employ our thoughts or speculation. Our present task is to perfect our present expression. It is not necessary that the child of Mars should change places with the Jovian; it *is* desirable that each should express his own horoscope properly. But our science tells us—and this is of vital importance—that each horoscope contains in some real sense every planet; and the Martian, while remaining Mars, must not therefore neglect Venus, nor the Venerean avoid the task of developing a true Martian characteristic. Ultimately we must unfold the meanings of all principles and become genuine Lords of the Zodiacal Wheel.

That it is possible for each of us to do this is evident from the fact that many have so attained, and what one can do others can also accomplish, being derived from one Source and therefore possessing similar potentialities.

Our relationship to the Zodiac is not that of creature to Creator; and although the influence of the stellar bodies is subtle in the extreme and has great power in regard to our bodies and fortunes, even invading our mental and emotional processes, there is no astrological proof that we are entirely dominated by it. If this were indeed the case it is probable that our prophecies would more often be true, though at the same time nothing could be more useless than the foreseeing of the inevitable. But any deterministic doctrine destroys the validity of all reasoning processes whatever, including the very process by which its adherents attempt to demonstrate its truth.

It is true that (to take an extreme example) a man with many planets in Taurus and Saturn in elevation in square to them, will not readily appreciate the beauty of abstract ideas, yet there is no reason why, in his own sphere (however limited it may be) he should not live a good and useful life.

There is indeed a Path for each, and here we return to the Triadic division, which we called the Modes of Action.

The three Paths described in Indian philosophy are those of Good Works, Devotion, and Understanding—*dharma, bhakta, and gnana marga.*

Each of these may be directed downward to the practical or upward to the ONE, and these are the karma and raja margas, bearing relation to the malefics and the benefics, which in a certain manner turn the influence of the astrological neutrals, the Sun, Moon, and Mercury, upwards or downwards.

The three margas are, of course, the three Modes, and the two orientations, upwards and downwards, may be likened to the twin polarities.

This may be expressed in diagram.

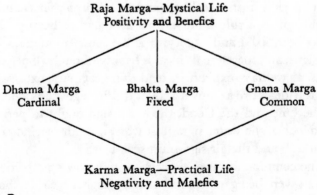

Raja Marga—Mystical Life
Positivity and Benefics

Dharma Marga   Bhakta Marga   Gnana Marga
Cardinal   Fixed   Common

Karma Marga—Practical Life
Negativity and Malefics

D

The Ideal Principle of the Cardinal Cross is *Goodness*, and is founded in the Will.

The Fixed Cross has as its Ideal *Beauty*, and appeals to our Taste or Heart.

The Common Cross has as its Ideal *Truth*, and appeals to our Reason, or Head.

The Elements may be related to the three Paths as follows: *Fire* symbolises the One, or the Divine Unity in which all are made whole and complete. *Earth* is related to Good Works, or Goodness. *Water* symbolises Beauty, for it is related to those parts of our nature to which the Beautiful specially appeals, that is, to the affections and emotions. *Air* is the triplicity of Truth.

Uniting the Elements and Modes in one Table we get a sort of double correspondence.

	Unity	Goodness	Truth	Beauty
Goodness	♈	♑	♎	♋
Beauty	♌	♉	♒	♍
Truth	♐	♍	II	♓

This Table may occasion some surprise, unless we recall that it sets out ideal correspondences, of which we often see the opposites in the world around us. Scorpio, for example, might not as a rule be described as a sign of beauty. But, being both fixed and watery, it is the most emotional of all the signs, and therefore its ideal is beauty, though all negative signs, as we have explained, tend to a pragmatic expression. But the ideals are as shown above: the fire signs should aspire to the One and the Good, the earth sign ought to perform good works, the water sign must worship at the shrine of the beautiful, and the air sign must seek truth.

The common forms of perversion may now be tabled, the ideas given being of course, merely suggestive. It should be noted that air and earth and fire and water are in a sense opposites; for example, an excess of air is much the same as a deficiency of earth, and so on.

	Excess	Deficiency	Misuse
Fire	Irresponsible	Dull	Profligate
	Excitable	Uninspired	Tyrannical
	Careless	Lack of Zeal	Self-willed
Earth	Sordid	Poor sense	Obstinate
	Stupid	"actuality"	Rude
	Inert	Unpractical	Churlish
Air	Fanciful	Unrefined	Subject to illusions
	Dreamy	Unsocial	
	Indolent	Without culture	
	Fickle		
Water	Morbid	Unsympathetic	Superstitious
	Over-emotional	Hard	Credulous
	Sensitive		Timorous
	Secretive		

Each of these can, of course, operate in any of the three Modes, and will then specially affect the will, feelings, or mind as the case may be. As a general rule we shall profit more by dwelling on the ideals themselves rather than by studying their distorted and mixed reflections in the lower aspects of human life: nevertheless, this last is the usual work of the astrologer.

It will be of interest to tabulate the Virtues of the Signs from the standpoint of the Modes and Triplicities. The Cardinal signs give us the four cardinal virtues of Plato:

Aries	.	.	.	.	Courage
Cancer	.	.	.	.	Prudence
Libra	.	.	.	.	Justice
Capricorn	.	.	.	.	Temperance

These are all phrases of Action. One will not act at all without courage, but courage without prudence would merely defeat its own ends and destroy itself. Libra demands

Justice or Moderation in action for the sake of others, and in order to obtain more effective action through cooperation, which a spirit of unfairness would render impossible. Capricorn, by calling for self-control and temperate behaviour in victory provides for the permanence of the results of action. In a sense Aries and Cancer each correct the tendencies of the other to excess and deficiency respectively, while Libra and Capricorn prevent inordinate expression.

Taurus	Integrity
Leo	Magnanimity
Scorpio	Fidelity
Aquarius	Veracity

It should be observed that we are now approaching these matters from the moral point of view and are tabulating ideals of conduct. Hence our process goes most easily with the cardinal signs, which have special reference to conduct. When we deal with the fixed signs we still find appropriate moral ideals, but they are ideals of feeling rather than action, and are largely based on emotion. Thus, by Veracity I mean rather the love of truth than the actual practice of truth, which is rather implied in the Libran ideal of Justice.

All the fixed signs have ideals of stability and dependability. Taurus is dependable because of its sincerity of purpose and dislike of uncertainty and change, and the fidelity of Scorpio is the same thing under a more intense aspect. Magnanimity, because it is not swayed by little things, is to be relied on, and the veracity of Aquarius makes it impartially just and incapable of hypocrisy.

Gemini	Insight
Virgo	Precision
Sagittary	Speculative Energy
Pisces	Emotional Understanding

It is not easy to ascribe strictly moral virtues to the Common signs, for they are, of course, pre-eminently mental, and their function is to arrange things, especially with a view to practical usefulness.

It is regrettable that an apparent misunderstanding of this function has led to their being called *flexible* or *adaptable* as if they were cunning time-servers behaving as best suits their purpose. They are in reality active adapters, not passively adaptable, although the two negatives may sometimes be too ready to suit their conduct to their company. They work hard, Gemini to use ideas and words, Virgo to use tools, Sagittary to explore both intellectually and as an actual traveller, mapping strange countries and so integrating the unknown, while Pisces adapts colours in painting and expression in the dramatic art.

To complete our work we should now turn from this study of the Good to the investigation of the astrological aspects of Beauty and Truth, and it might be possible to do this successfully. But in a sense the cardinal signs and their special relation to the Good may be taken as standards for all three Paths, and enough has been said, both here and in other works, to indicate clearly how these further developments may be successfully pursued in compliance with Zodiacal science.

Saturn is particularly the planet of the True, Venus of the Beautiful, and Jupiter of the Good, but the final union of the Soul with its Father, accomplished by the spontaneous uplifting of all its faculties, would seem to be the work of Neptune.

V

A FINAL INQUIRY

Since most of us seek to use our astrological knowledge practically, in other words, to investigate the actual meaning of horoscopes, it will be of interest to inquire how far we can safely predicate the true condition of the Soul from a nativity and in what ways this can be done.

The opinion is offered that the Soul, interiorly moved by its spiritual aspect, acts upon and in some degree becomes enmeshed in material conditions, including the body, as a result of its inherent movement towards self-unfoldment. For, as we have said, the Soul is self-perpetuating and self-progressive, and, furthermore, it seeks to become self-knowing. That, indeed, as the Delphic Oracle said, is its main business. To know itself truly it must encounter that which is directly opposite to itself, for we cannot know our strength by merely tensing our muscles, but by straining them against those of an antagonist or against something inanimate. So the soul can never know itself by pure intro-spection, but by contrasting itself with what is not itself. The soul, in its higher aspect, is incontaminate and superior to any sort of corruption, but it can and does, by descending into matter, evolve certain lower aspects by which it acts on matter and even becomes fastened therein, as a tree grows

47

roots and becomes fixed in earth. For example, having once formed a physical body, the soul is forced to find physical nutriment for it, and so necessarily forms an attachment to food, clothing, shelter, and other things that the body needs. And, since the body is useful to it in its quest for self-gnosis, this attachment is perfectly right, except when the soul forgets itself, identifies itself with its body, and develops a fever, as it were, lest the supports of the body should prove insufficient. It is manifest, I think, that the inordinate aspect is due to the body attributing not some, but too much, value to physical things, and the question will inevitably arise as to how this error can come about, since there seems no reason why the soul should not enter material conditions and yet retain a memory of its true nature sufficient to prevent its becoming attached to these beyond what is right and needful. Philosophy has propounded several answers to this question, but it seems to me that, whatever it might develop in this manner, it could never develop a real sense of *power* except by combating something. And, since it cannot fight against itself, it turns against material conditions and against other souls, which it could not do unless it did to some extent forget its real nature, for, except for so doing, it would regard other souls as its brothers and material things as its subjects and playthings. Thus it becomes attached to worldly objects both in the way of hate and love.

Again, it is not hard to think that a constant recollection of its primal happiness would act as a deterrent and encumbrance in its work in matter, just as a good soldier, in the Great War, had to forget civilian occupations and throw himself into his new life.

Between its lives on earth the soul probably returns to a condition more similar to its own nature, and even evil men,

I should imagine, having left their bodies, would in this way enjoy some respite and opportunity for recovery. But when having thus recuperated itself, the spiritual impulse towards fresh experience and unfoldment becomes potent once more, then it will descend into a body at a time when the celestial conditions resemble itself, its wishes, choice, and aspirations. So, if it has failed before to attain a true balance in the body between the physical and spiritual, it will probably go down with a renewed desire to master its lesson and will come into birth at a time when the horoscope will be appropriate to such a destiny, and similar—not indeed to itself, for it is in its pure aspect insusceptible of much that a horoscope of birth denotes—but to its choice as regards terrestrial things and to its state of development in reference to the incarnate existence, wherein it falls into the realm of time and space and becomes capable of being described in terms of these categories.

It therefore would follow that the Nativity indicates the general destiny of the life, for the soul, once incarnate, cannot reverse its choice. Further, although a nativity cannot represent the condition of the soul in its extra-spatial and supra-temporal state, it can represent its present relation to material things and its possible psychological reactions. It is in fact the record of its past successes and failures in its attempts to adapt itself to an alien condition. Self-consciousness and intelligence, and pain too, result from an acute perception of its essential unlikeness to that which is around it, and therefore we say that evil aspects denote vigour of mind and sometimes even of body.

The greatest difficulty of practical astrology, I think, is to differentiate between what will affect character and what will work out in terms of destiny, as for instance, loss of health, position, money, or other possessions. Frequently the same aspect appears to affect both. Certain technical rules have been given, but they are not infallible.

Now this problem arises because the soul, by identifying itself, so far as it can, with matter and thus living a sensuous life, or even an intelligent but unenlightened one, ceases to feel bad aspects acutely, being no longer aware of what they really denote, which is the fact of its being in a state foreign to its real nature. Therefore the aspects tend to operate, as we say, in terms of character, and this becomes debased, while fortune and health may be excellent. Sometimes the soul struggles intermittently, and then bad aspects may work in both ways; and sometimes, having a clear recollection of what it is and what its circumstances mean, it returns to its native purity of character, but, having made an irrevocable choice so far as this life is concerned, ill-health and misfortune may pursue its path. This occurs, perhaps, most often of all in those cases when the individual, having as it were suddenly wakened to the true nature and destiny of the soul, goes to an excess of spirituality and neglects the duties of the physical life altogether, caring neither for health nor money, a condition common when Neptune occupies certain positions.

When we view the question in this light we see why it is often very hard to decide what is incorrectly called "the age of the soul." It is a question, not of age, but of self-realisation; and this may come at any moment and alter the entire tenor of the horoscope, throwing the operation of an aspect or of several aspects from one plane to another. I do not say for one moment that a change of this nature, called in some circles conversion, will occur without directional influences of an appropriate nature, but it would be a matter of considerable delicacy of judgment to foretell when this would happen, or even that an event of that kind would happen at all. We are still in that state of ignorance that even the best astrologer may foresee a long sea voyage in place of a spiritual initiation: Sun in trine to Neptune, in the majority of cases, might equally mean either, so far as most of us can see.

Our difficulties arise from the fact that the real causes of things happen out of our sight; we see only effects. Again, all discussion of the soul and its problems is made difficult by the fact that it is essentially beyond space and time, and yet, from our point of view, exists within these categories. Hence all that we can say of it is likely to be paradoxical. The soul is, indeed, the greatest of mysteries, yet by patient thought we can get nearer and nearer to an understanding of what it is, and such an understanding gradually throws light on the Astrology of the soul. But each soul is a secret to itself, and it is impossible for us to judge why each individual has chosen the nativity that it has chosen and the life which it has elected to face. It must, by its essential character, unfold itself in every possible way, or, in a word, it must grow, and, since it views these matters from beyond time, it probably cares little about the exact amount of happiness or unhappiness that will fall to its lot in each particular birth. Once in matter, its old mistakes and weaknesses come to life, as it were, and its pure vision is obscured.

It is then that it is liable to develop the various inordinate tendencies which are best classified under the four elements. These we have discussed already in relation to Goodness, but we may now briefly consider them from the point of view of the mystic.[1]

[1] I use the word "mystic" as denoting one who seeks union with the Divine by the upliftment of all the faculties, including the intellectual. Many limit the word to those who are, as it is expressed, on the heartside. But such men as Plato and Plotinus were examples of the highest intellectual development.

Fire is characterised by a tendency to too much emotional development, at the expense of the other side of the nature. Thus, such characters soar high, but often fall equally low, and, from too great a straining upward, there may be grave relapses to what is called the "Dark Night of the Soul" and similar experiences, such as are described in the manual *Light on the Path*. In the worst cases sensuality may appear as a result of sudden failure to maintain an unnaturally high and at the same time unbalanced condition. Many men of notorious immorality have been pseudo-mystics of this class. *Water* is an element which seems to be strangely attracted towards phenomenalism, that is, the seeking for signs and wonders and the various phenomena of the spiritist and self-styled magician, which are either pure deception or are, in actuality, very different from what they are represented as being. These matters may be legitimately investigated by those who desire to study the laws and existences of the astral world in a scientific spirit, but they have no relation at all to true religion or mysticism.

In Astrology both these elements produce special types of students. Fire is the element of the wild and irresponsible prophet, whose chief interest in our science appears to be to attempt to make "lucky hits." Shoot often enough and you can hit anything within range, and these ardent prognostics employ a sort of astrological machine-gun, peppering the future with red-letter days in the not unreasonable hope that one at least will coincide with some dismal fatality—plague, earthquake, or war. Water introduces us to those who endeavour to investigate past lives, for water loves the past as fire loves the future. It is possible that a knowledge of these matters may be given to some, and it is even within the bounds of the possible that we may be able to determine

accurately from one natus the character and thus the date of
the last and of the next. But most of what has been published
about the past lives of individuals is obviously tainted with
egotism, sometimes of a repellent or ridiculous kind, writers
giving themselves the names of heroes and demi-gods, while
fixing their antagonists with far less attractive soubriquets!
Fantasy can easily run riot in these fruitless speculations, but
a more healthy tendency will concern itself with present
problems and the work that is immediately at hand rather
than with our vicissitudes of many centuries ago.

Earth is an element which tends to too great pragmatism,
"good works" being regarded as the essential, while the inner
life is neglected, and the ideal of "commonsense religion" is
allowed to expel the more delicate and profounder aspects of
the Ascent. Such things are the highest manifestation of
earth and are, of course, of the utmost practical importance,
but they are essentially Mars–Saturn in nature.

Air has as its inordinate aspect a relatively too great devotion to intellectualism, resulting in a purely philosophical
view of religion and a tendency to regard all religio-psycho-
logical phenomena as subjects for rigid and abstract classification; whereas the soul is a living thing, which cannot be
reduced to strict measurement or treated as if it were purely
static without misleading results.

In Astrology the earth-tendency produces those to whom
the science has only the aspect of a practical art, in a word, it
is the art of delineating horoscopes, natal and horary, and
usually from the point of view of fate rather than growth and
freedom. Practical Astrology is at present of only limited
use, because our knowledge of it is so imperfect, but, with
increasing understanding, it will be recognised as one of the
supremely useful arts and one of the most valuable branches

of knowledge known to man. Nevertheless the utilitarian standard, by itself, produces a wrong attitude of mind.

Air, in Astrology, may be taken to correspond to the "unco guid" among us, to whom any practical use of the science is unworthy and tainted with "black magic." It is obvious that astrology *could* be used in a dishonourable manner, and as our knowledge grows this possibility will become more and more dangerous, unless astrology becomes also so widely practised that all can have its assistance. Even thus, it is probable that evil magical practices would be immensely fortified by astrological knowledge. But these dangers do not justify us in studying Astrology simply as a theoretical science, or, if we choose to do so, we need not look down upon those who are more immediately practical in their views. On the face of it, the use of astrology neither makes a dishonest action better, nor an honest one worse.

The true scope of Astrology is a most important and a much debated matter.

According to the philosophy on which the present work is based we may ascribe validity to the horoscope in regard to all material matters, including one's so-called luck and fate, one's inherited tendencies, position, money, physical body, and general environment. In psychology all that is usually called temperament is denoted in the nativity and the secondary maps, such as epochs, of which we hear much, but as to which there is very little clear agreement. But the lower one descends from universal principles the more widely differentiated does everything tend to become, until we get the most trifling incidents, minor peculiarities of conduct, little turns of speech, and so forth. These reflect planetary action, often quite clearly. But universal principles have no liability in respect of planetary influences; they are immutable and eternal Realities, and it is from them that the characters of the planets are derived. By uniting himself with these man becomes himself rooted in the Unchanging, and, although he may certainly retain traces of astrological influences, yet the more nearly he approaches the perfect Ideals, the less is he characterised by the merely personal and separative. His nativity then becomes a register of certain relationships between himself and the material cosmos, which, indeed, the world at large may consider of paramount importance, but which will mean very little to him. Mars, Saturn, and Uranus, the lords of this world, may indeed assail him, but they will inflict only passing annoyance, as banditti may harass the baggage-train of an army, but dare not face the disciplined soldiers in battle.

VI

THE ZODIAC AND THE ART OF DIRECTING

FROM the point of view of practical astrology the most valuable part of our investigation will perhaps be that which deals with the Zodiac as a basis of directing, that is, of foretelling the times in the life when the indications of the natal map will come into open manifestation. Without a reliable and complete system of directing all natal astrology tends to remain vague and abstract, yet all candid astrologers will admit that none of our present systems gives entirely satisfactory results. Some are reliable as far as they go, at least in most cases, but while their positive side is accurate, within certain wide limits, their negative aspects are uncertain. Thus a given direction may as a rule operate, but events of importance occur without any corresponding indication. On the other hand, some systems simply do not appear to work on occasion, and a serious direction, which may have caused much concern to the native, passes without any ruffle in the smooth surface of existence, or, more frequently, a good direction is inoperative.

I believe that these defects are due to the fact that nearly all systems, and certainly *all* that have been in use until very recent times, have been *astronomical*, by which I mean that

they are based on astronomical movements of the bodies of
the Solar System, actual or apparent.[1]

Now, being based on data of the physical plane they
operate with uncertainty, and may, of course, be defeated by
other factors belonging to the same plane.

To get reliability we must seek a system that is based on
something superior to the physical plane and is therefore
only to a secondary extent liable to modification by it.

This must be a *symbolic* system, that is, it has a real basis,
resting on universal principles, and must deal with the reflected action of these principles in matter.

Then, again, it is not open to question, so far as some of us
are concerned, that every body in the horoscope, as well as
the M.C., can be directed forward in the Zodiac at the rate of
$1°$ per annum, and that very valuable directions arise in this
manner. For instance, in Nurse Cavell's horoscope, given on
p. 99, we see that the dangerous configuration is in the double
opposition (☽ ☌ ♅) ☍ (☿ ☌ ♃). Venus is ruler of the VIII.
If to the four bodies mentioned we add $50°$ we bring them all
close to the square of Venus. Nurse Cavell was about two
months under fifty years of age when executed.

This method of direction differs from the *radix system*, which
uses the mean daily motion of the Sun, and is more trouble-
some to use, and yet, in my personal experience, not so
accurate.

Similar direction can also be made in *right ascension*, with
excellent results, the bodies being taken both with and without latitude. But this, of course, is a purely astronomical
method, based on actual apparent motion.

---

[1] Apparent motion is, of course, real motion. Its apparency consists in
the fact that it is different from what it appears to be. The apparent
motion of the Sun is due to the actual motion of the Earth.

It is strange that for many centuries these simple methods have been overlooked, while many complex systems have flourished, although it is extremely doubtful if they are in the least better than these.[1]

By these methods direction can be made to the cusps, provided these are accurately determined. *Per contra*, it can be used as a means of rectification.

For example, if I may include some personal examples, I have Uranus in 12.24 ♎ and Jupiter in 5.20 ♏. The difference is 22.56, dating to beginning of January, 1910. That year was full of Jupiter influences, including my first introduction to Astrology. My Sun, in 11.49 ♒, is 23.31 from the trine of this planet, which dates almost exactly to this fortunate occurrence. Jupiter to cusp III is 39.40, dating almost exactly to the first issue of *Astrology*.

My experience with these systems is that the symbolic method is more psychological in effect and sometimes produces *obvious* effects some time after exactitude; on the other hand, the same directions calculated in right ascension work extremely close to time; in fact, as a rule they are within a very few days indeed of the exact arc.

I believe that these methods, together with the unquestionably useful lunar secondaries, constitute a pretty

---

[1] However, since the above was written, the *solar arc* method has gained considerable vogue on the Continent.

In this, the actual progression of the Sun, by secondary direction, is used. This may vary considerably from the one-degree increment since the apparent daily motion of the Sun changes with the time of year, being much slower in summer than in winter.

It is only necessary to find the progressed position of the Sun, to subtract from it the natal solar position, and apply the resultant solar arc to all bodies and points that it is desired to progress.

It is apparent that this method has much to commend it.

complete guide to the life *once the map is properly rectified*. I emphasise this, for in my opinion directions to and by the angles are of very first importance, but, of course, until the horoscope has been rectified neither these nor any cusps can be used.

Transits and lunar secondaries are of great use as indices of the exact day on which directions will operate. Pre-natal or converse secondaries are, I believe, unreliable, and I am disposed to think that their supposed action is often only the effect of a coinciding direction in right ascension, or some other influence that dates to the same time.

But while the One-degree and related Systems go a long way to satisfy requirements, the $1°$ of longitude method is capable of a most interesting extension, which may prove to be of appreciable value.

This extension, combined with the method of progression at the rate of $1°$ of longitude, I call the *Fractional System*.

This is founded on the thesis that the distance at birth in longitude between any two bodies, which is called the *basic arc*, and which is, of course, an arc of direction between them in the One-degree System, is symbolic of the mutual relationship existing throughout the life between them, even if there is no recognised aspect between them.

Furthermore, this basic arc, which stands, so to speak, for the major "beat" as between the two bodies in question, may be split up into minor "beats" which represent the space in time between each successive manifestation of their combined influence. These minor beats I call sub-arcs, and they are obtained by dividing the basic arc so as to obtain various fractional parts, such as halves, quarters, eighths, and so on. Or, if the basic arc is small, then we may similarly multiply by 2, $2\frac{1}{2}$, 3, $3\frac{1}{2}$, and so on.

If we wish to find the influences at work in any one year we can easily do so. Suppose the year corresponds to age forty-one. Then we must add to each planetary position and to the cusps 41°, 20°.30′, 10°.15′, 51°.15′, 61°.30′, and 82°. We can, of course, extend our arcs in either direction, but naturally the lesser beats are of minor importance.

The most important arcs are those actually between two bodies, or between a body and a cusp. An arc from a body to a place of aspect, although a legitimate arc of direction in itself, does not so readily lend itself to fractional treatment. Thus, Moon in 7.24′ ♉ to the square of Mars in 0.26′ Ⅱ would be a good direction of 23.02′. But if we add to this one quarter (5.45)′, obtaining 28.47′, this might be found to have little or no effect.

Some illustrations will soon demonstrate the simplicity of the method.

Take General Gordon's death at age fifty-two. He had Mars in 1°♉ and Moon in 27°♉. The basic arc is therefore 26, and the double arc 52.

Nurse Cavell had 50° between Mars and asct., and this gives her death at 50. She had 34° between Saturn and Sun, so that a 1½ arc is 51. Mars to opposition Moon is 26, of which the double arc is 52.

For serious events several directions may be found, and the exact time of incidence must be sought in transits, lunations, and lunar secondaries. In these directions it seems that the effect is that of a conjunction (even when we direct to an opposition, as above). Therefore we judge the result from the intrinsic characters of the planets and their sympathy or antipathy the one with the other.

Passing to some further examples, Rupert Brooke died at about twenty-eight years of age from sunstroke on military service. His nativity is given on p. 84, and the following arcs may easily be checked.

Sun to Uranus is 58, half of which is 29°.

Mars to Sun is 26°.

Saturn to Sun is 13, double which is 26°.

Sun to opp. Neptune is 109, quarter which is $27\frac{1}{4}$°.

Moon conj. Neptune, the same.

Moon opp. Uranus is 59, half of which is $29\frac{1}{2}$°.

This constitutes a fairly formidable list of evil influences. But we may go further in our search for evil hylegiacal indices. To Mars add $19\frac{1}{2}$ and we get it opposition the asc. To $19\frac{1}{2}$ add half itself, and we get $29\frac{1}{4}$, which is fairly near, in view of the ascending sign being one of quick motion. Similarly a small rectification will give us M.C. 4° ♐, from which to opp. Saturn is 54, half of which is 27.

Case 7, on p. 103, has as its worst aspect Sun square Neptune, and the difference between these bodies is 84. Half this figure is close to death. Mars and Sun are 56 apart, and three-quarters of this gives 42. Death often precedes the exactitude of a direction, because the body gives way before the utmost tension has been applied.

William Blake died aged seventy, the exact arc between Sun and Saturn (in VIII). Mars to Venus (in VI) is 140, of which half is 70. Moon to Mars is 47, $1\frac{1}{2}$ of which is $70\frac{1}{2}$. There are several other serious directions within a space of two years of death.

William Stead died at the age of sixty-three. By $\frac{1}{2}$ arc Neptune was close to Saturn and to the squares thrown by that planet to the Lights and Mercury. Jupiter, lord VIII, is within a degree of the opposition of Uranus by basic arc. By $\frac{1}{2}$ arc Mercury is near square Mars and Mars near square Neptune. By double arc (126°) Neptune is in 11° ♋, an obviously dangerous position. It is true that the Moon, by basic arc, is sextile the Sun, but, being in opposition at birth, this configuration could not save.

I trust that the above examples will tell the reader all there is at present to know about this system, some inklings of which I have had in mind for a year or so, but which I have only recently investigated sufficiently to embolden me to lay it before the astrological world as a contribution towards the symbological aspect of the Science. I hope that it will arouse some interest and may even achieve something towards the permanent elucidation of our directional difficulties, which have generated a weltering *melee* of conflicting practices. I would warn students not to judge fractional directions too separatively; it is necessary to calculate all the important arcs for a period, and to judge them collectively. It is very often impossible, or, at any rate very misleading, to try to take life to pieces; it is an organic whole, and so, too, in a true directional system all the parts are interlocked. Subject to this the system is very simple and easily tested, but it is highly probable that a great deal may yet be discovered about it. For instance, it may well be found that each fraction has its own character.

The real trouble with Directional Astrology is not so much the difficulty of finding the correct system and rejecting the incorrect as to find the best from among numerous methods, of which all appear to have at least a moderate amount of truth and practical advantage. It is hardly to be doubted that (leaving the astronomical systems out of the question) valid symbolic systems can be founded upon *all* the primary, and some compound, numbers. Numbers are at the basis of all things. Or, if we prefer to say so, the basis of all things can be numerically expressed. This is none the less true because of the existence of numerological systems which are obviously mere caricatures of science.

In Astrology the chief numbers, from a practical point of view, are of course two, three, four, and twelve. It may be asked why, having divided the Circle of the Zodiac into twelve, we then divide the twelfths into 30° each? Some writers have, not unreasonably, questioned the validity of the degree as a genuine natural division and have claimed that the signs should be redivided into twelfths of $2\frac{1}{2}°$ each.

On this theory I have based the *Duodenary System* of directing, in which each body is moved $2\frac{1}{2}°$ to the year, and very striking results can be derived from this simple and rational measure. To find the time at which any arc will act it is only necessary to divide it by $\frac{2}{5}$; and, similarly, to find the arc for any year of life it is only necessary to multiply that year by 5 and add that result to all bodies.

For example, Rupert Brooke, whose nativity is given on p. 84, died at about twenty-eight years of age. This age, multiplied by $\frac{5}{2}$, equals seventy. Adding this figure to Neptune we bring it to conjunction the Sun. Adding it to Mars, we bring it to Venus, ruling the eighth. Adding it to Saturn, we bring it to Uranus, in the eighth. Adding it to the Sun, we bring it to the eighth house, in square to the mid-point between the two malefics in the sixth. Adding it to the ascendant, we bring it to the square of Mars. I doubt if any other system will produce more appropriate results.

In Nurse Cavell's case fifty years of age means an arc of 125°, and this brings all four of the dangerous bodies, Moon, Mercury, Jupiter, and Uranus, into conflict with Saturn by major evil aspect, the Sun being near the opposition of the radical ascendant.

In Case 7 the nativity of a woman who died at the age of forty-one (equalling an arc of 102½°), we find Saturn conjunction with Uranus in the sixth in mutables—she died of pneumonia. Mars is opposite the radical ascendant. Mercury is opposed to Saturn, a most significant aspect. The Moon forms a grand trine with Uranus and Neptune, a strange configuration, reminding us that she had sought to take her own life and apparently desired to die. Saturn is close to the square of the radical eighth house.

Blake died at the age of seventy, when his Sun had just passed the square of Mars and the opposition of Mercury, being exactly square to Jupiter.

Stead was sixty-three, equalling an arc of about 157°. Mars goes from opposition Saturn to square the Sun (less than 1°). Saturn is past the sextile of the Sun, but this aspect is in any case vitiated by the radical square. Uranus is going to the square of Mercury and opposition of Saturn (about 4½°). The ascendant is square Uranus. The M.C. has the same aspects as Uranus, but closer. Venus is in opposition to Mars (about 0½° apart).

We can move the Houses as in the ordinary progressed horoscope. Thus the progressed M.C. being 5½° ♎, the progressed ascendant, under the latitude of birth, is 3½° ♐, which is going to the square of Neptune. This, in fact, is the worst aspect of all as far as drowning is concerned.

But the whole directional position is appalling. In addition to the above, Jupiter is square Uranus, and its trine to Venus radical is vitiated by the natal square.

With these few examples we may leave the Duodenary System to the mercy of the host of critics who delight, as the author himself delights, in testing and retesting such propositions, both practically and theoretically. It was not originally intended to publish anything on the subject for some time to come, but I have decided to offer it for what it may be worth, convinced that at any rate from the theoretical side it stands fairly secure, being founded on that profound twelvefold principle, the significance of which it has been the chief aim of this work to explain. For that reason this system is in a sense more germane to our present investigations than the Fractional.

VII

ON TRANSITS

VERY little has been written about Transits, either here or abroad.

The reason probably is, that most astrologers consider there is not much to be said on this subject, owing to its simplicity.

No calculations are involved and there are hardly any points in dispute.

Another probable reason for lack of attention, so far as writings are concerned, is that transits are commonly thought to be of comparatively little importance, referring chiefly, if not entirely, to the least significant events of life.

In reply one might say that perhaps transits are not quite as simple as they appear. At any rate, they repay a certain amount of study such as is not always vouchsafed to them.

Answering the second reason, one may affirm that even if transits were concerned only with minor matters, still such things, if individually trivial, make up for this in being very frequent; they are always with us. Again, it may be said that, so far as learning about the planets goes, one can do this just as well from small events as from those that are of epoch-making importance in the life.

For example, if one is sufficiently interested and methodical to keep a register of transits, it is often very illuminating to watch (let us say) the transits of Mars over the same natal point, roughly every two years. One can note the essential similarities underlying outward differences and thus acquire a better knowledge of the value both of the planet in transit and the body subject to transit.

This cannot be done with ordinary directions, for even the progressed Moon will not pass the same spot more often than thrice in the average life.

But are transits, in and by themselves, only capable of producing or indicating the lesser occasions of life?

It is admitted in classic astrology that transits can appear important, but only because they sometimes act as excitants of a direction by forming contact, at a time when this direction is approximately exact, with the bodies involved in this direction.

It is usually implied that transits *by themselves* can do little.

This question cannot really be answered because there are so many systems of directing current at the present time. They have proliferated almost alarmingly of late years and each and every one has its enthusiastic supporters.

Thus if I assert that at such and such a time an important event occurred and that there were only transits to indicate it, it is quite certain that some such advocate will step forward and declare that his system, if none other, admirably meets the requirements of the occasion.

The adherent of transits may maintain that *these*, at any rate, form a compact system, easy to understand and use, that they may be tested almost daily, and, furthermore, that their rationale is not difficult to accept. Those who are ignorant of the more abstruse laws of nature, or who decry them, find comfort in transits, which lend themselves to some extent to an explanation acceptable to a materialistic point of view which rejects reference to such things as the Law of Correspondences as vague and unproven. And it is upon this law that most, if not all, directional systems properly so called depend. The physicist will not be impressed by statements such as that one day of life is reflected in the year or that one degree of the ecliptic has a similar value.

Now as to the assertion that transits are chiefly if not entirely concerned with trivia, there is certainly room here for comment.

Generally, the effectiveness of a transit depends upon the speed of the transitting body and the sensitiveness of the point under transit, especially in relation to the body that forms the transit.

An analogy will illustrate this.

A quick transit, as by the Sun, Mercury or Venus, over a point by a body that has no powerful natal relation to the body or point under transit may be likened to two people passing one another in the street, neither being acquainted with the other.

But if the transit is quick but the two bodies concerned have a natal relationship, then this may be likened to two friends passing each other. Both are in a hurry—or at any rate one is—but, since they are known to each other, they nod or give expression to their friendship.

On the other hand, if the transit is a slow one, either because the planet is temporarily slow of motion or because its apparent motion is always slow, and, most of all, if the planet in transit is stationary on the other, then this resembles two people meeting and stopping for a talk, amicable or otherwise. From this conversation important things may develop.

To give a personal instance, the writer has a close natal square between Venus and Neptune.

Therefore even the transit of Venus, though quickly formed and dissolved, invariably produces a distinct effect. Its station on Neptune would be much stronger. The transit of Neptune over Venus would probably mark a distinctly significant period in the life, all the more so if it recurred by reason of retrogression.

Even the older astrologers, who were devotees of the so called primary system of directing and usually had little to say of anything else, acknowledged that a station, particularly of the outer planets, could be important.

Naturally the closer the station is to the radical point, the stronger will the correlated events be, and if there is a radical relationship between planet in transit and point under transit, the phenomenon will once again increase in significance.

Hence a glance through the ephemeris for each coming year should certainly take note of any significant stations.

Thus we find, in August 1939, a station of Saturn at 1° 16' of Taurus, within 28' of Hitler's radical Sun, and this is followed, in December, by another station of the same planet about 1° from his natal Mercury.

But in January 1945 there is a station of Neptune which is only 2' from the square of his radical Moon, and, note further, while Neptune is stationary at 6° 26' Libra, his Moon being in 6° 28' Capricorn, Saturn is, on the day of station, in 6° 30' Cancer. Surely an advocate of transits might say that this is a sufficiently serious configuration to match the conditions of the times as they affected the Fuehrer.

It must be a rule of all prediction that rare events must be shown by rare configurations. One cannot account for death and downfall by something that occurs quite frequently in the heavens.

This example fulfils the condition.

In August 1940, when the invasion of Britain was in the balance, Saturn was stationary at 14° 47′ of Taurus, near Hitler's Venus and Mars and in square to Saturn.

Possibly it was because of this formation that his astrologers advised him against invasion. What would have happened had he persisted we can only surmise. One cannot usefully conjecture about might-have-beens. We know what happened, or did not happen.

Saturn is important in every map, but in Hitler's case its predominance over the whole nativity is obvious.

We have, for simplicity's sake, written only of transits over natal positions but the same rules apply to similar passages of bodies over progressed positions, though, with the slow-moving points, the difference in time will not be great.

This, however, adds to the importance of a transit. If my natal and progressed Saturn, for example, are within a degree or two of each other, the transits over the two will follow one another quickly and will mean a double excitation of whatever they may portend, pleasant or otherwise. If the latter, then it may be likened to two blows in quick succession. One receives the second before one has had time to recover from the first.

We may now consider three matters which have an important bearing on the use of transits for prediction:

(1) Several transits may have no inter-relationship but may occur around the same time and have a generally similar significance.

Thus in one part of the natus we may find Jupiter in favourable transit and in another, Venus.

Such concurrence in time may naturally indicate a well-marked period, according to the nature of the indications.

(2) There may be what we will call a multiple transit when more than one body, at the same time, affect a single point.

A common case is that of lunations and those special lunations which are eclipses. At that time both Sun and Moon are at the same point and may therefore both simultaneously be in contact with a third.

In July 1953 there was an eclipse of the Sun at 18½ Cancer and at the same time Uranus was in 18¾ Cancer and Mars in 18 Cancer. Saturn and Neptune were in close conjunction in Libra in square to the locus of the eclipse.

Thus we see that no less than *six* bodies were involved and any person whose nativity was closely affected by such an exceptional bombardment would almost certainly feel the effects in no uncertain way, either at the time or shortly thereafter.

Naturally one would agree that the concurrence of helpful directions might mitigate the outcome, just as that of difficult directions would aggravate conditions.

Moreover, it is commonsense to realize that all people do not and cannot respond to stellar influences alike. Both temperaments and circumstances differ. The same stroke which will flatten clay will have little effect upon a block of wood and less still upon a stone.

(3) Certain *times* add greatly to the effect of transits.

The present writer is sure that the Capricorn Ingress is of importance for the whole succeeding twelve months, coming into effect probably a month or so before the actual solstice.

Now should this map show strong transits to the natus under consideration, then these also will affect the native strongly, for good or ill as the case may be, during the ensuing year, though most strongly during the first quarter of that period.

It is not considered that the other three cardinal ingresses have the same value, and the ingresses into the fixed and mutable signs are probably less important still. Yet they are doubtless not without significance.

The student may observe the transits to Hitler's nativity at the 1944 winter ingress, and in particular the close opposition of Venus, his ruler, to his Saturn, and the almost exact square of Neptune to his Moon, which, if we use equal house division, ruled his 10th house.

There are no such significant transits in the map for the spring ingress, 1945, which immediately preceded his fall and death.

We may carry this further—and to an important consideration.

Let us turn to the winter ingress of 1888, which preceded the birth of this evil man.

Is it not remarkable that we find Mars in 15° of Aquarius, making up a most disastrous "T" square with his natal positions of Mars–Venus–Saturn?

It may be objected that thousands were born on the same day as Hitler and many must have had genitures that would appear virtually identical with his.

We shall pay some attention and make some suggestions with respect to this problem, so vital to a demonstration of the truth of Astrology, in the next chapter.

Meantime we have aimed at showing that Transits merit attention, both from the point of view of practical predictive work and as throwing light upon astrological principles.

In the old days, when there were only two known planets with a relatively slow apparent motion, it is understandable

F

that they should seem of small value. The discoveries of Uranus, Neptune, and Pluto have altered the position entirely; and it may be that, with the possible discovery of other planets with yet slower motion, it will be possible to rely upon transits and transits only, intelligently studied, to be our guides to future events.

VIII

PASTURES NEW

It is a common but obvious fallacy to condemn a subject as nonsense because nonsense is written about it. Judged by such a standard, many serious and important matters would stand convicted.

Certainly a great deal of nonsense has been written and published about what is called Numerology—a mongrel word and Arithmology would be preferable, but one that has apparently found its way into the dictionaries.

It may be asserted that very little indeed that has been penned on this topic would survive a critical examination, and it is quite probable that for every one case that has been cited to prove its value, a dozen could easily be found that would equally well tell against it.

Hence many people, even among those versed in the arcane wisdom, will repudiate all systems of numerology that have been publicly promulgated, even though none of them would for one moment reject the significance of numbers properly apprehended and applied.

The present writer has devoted much time to Numerology, used in conjunction with Astrology, and he is completely convinced that a field of the utmost value lies here, explaining among other things, why people with very similar nativities may have different lives and, to some extent, divergent dispositions.

Certainly this is not always so, nor is the explanation always hard to find when it is.

It has been shown by competent astrologers that persons, unrelated by blood but entering this world at the same time, or nearly so, often do have striking similarities of character and of destiny.

But it has also been shown that such differences as occur may often be explained by the *Law of Subsumption*: every natus can only be *fully* understood when it is considered in relation to the family map, the national and racial maps and also, in all likelihood, to the map of the vocation, where this is clear-cut.

All such maps cannot of course be obtained, but some can.

For instance, the destinies of members of the Royal Air Force might be studied in relation to the map of that Service; and the national maps of many countries are available.

Likewise the horoscopes of many great corporations and other commercial and financial enterprises are available. Such would undoubtedly often explain why a clever and able and industrious man may fail with one firm while less gifted individuals succeed.

Further, besides these more or less permanent horoscopes, there are those that are in action, if one may put it so, at the time of birth.

Thus there are the Great Conjunctions, notably those of Jupiter and Saturn, which are well known to have considerable value as indices of the periods they cover. It would probably be a fruitful field of investigation to see how far these might serve to explain the prominence or otherwise of individuals born during their terms of operation.

It is certain that the winter ingress prior to birth stamps its imprint, as it were, upon all that happens during the ensuing twelve months, and of this we have already spoken.

There is the classical case of Siamese twins, one of whom married and had children, while the other remained single.

It would be fair to dismiss such cases as freaks, things outside the order of nature which cannot be explained by ordinary laws and do not invalidate them.

But when all is said and done, we may return to our original suggestion that names have a true significance, and may be treated according to a valid system of numbers, and combined with each nativity in such a way as to give it a greater degree of individuality.

Several systems of correlation between letters and numbers have been used; but some appear to lack a reasonable foundation.

Why should a supposed system of Pythagoras have any validity for the English language?

The most rational system, one would suppose, would be to number the letters as they come in the alphabet of the language concerned. A would equal 1, Z would equal 26, in English.

This method seems not without a sound basis of fact.

However, as an astrologer the writer also uses a duodecimal system, thus:

1	2	3	4	5	6	7	8	9	10	11	12
A	B	C	D	E	F	G	H	I	J	K	L
M	N	O	P	Q	R	S	T	U	V	W	X
Y	Z										

This system he has subjected to rigid tests and he is convinced it has value.

In some fields it holds the key, or at any rate *a* key, to secrets after which many astrologers have sought but which lie outside the scope of a book such as this and are of such a nature that the present writer will certainly never commit them to print, lest they be put to unworthy uses by those who have not earned a title to this knowledge. The moral standards of astrologers are, on the whole, high and idealistic, but there are always those who seek easy money and perhaps still more who have an insatiable desire for personal kudos.

By way of exemplifying how, as I think, the above systems may be applied to personal maps we may take some of the cases given herein—selected, we would point out, long before such ideas were in the writer's mind.

Rupert Brooke evaluates at 68.

Cusps are somewhat problematical save in cases wherein the time of birth may be regarded as reasonably certain. But here we find 68 bringing Saturn to cusp 8, from the 6th house—a clear pointer to illness and early death.

Mercury comes to Uranus and Neptune to the Sun—indications of literary genius.

Shelley is 99—cusp 8 to square Pluto in 2nd. Certainly compatible with the renunciation of inheritance. Sun and Venus, being on cusp 8, give a tragic note. Worse still, Saturn comes to these conjunctions.

Poetic genius is shown clearly enough from the natus as it stands.

As an example of the method which gives each number its value according to its alphabetical place, we may take William Blake. Here we get a total of 110, bringing Neptune to the close conjunction of Jupiter and the Sun.

The duodecimal method makes Emily Popejoy equal 58 —Pluto on the ascendant, while the longer system yields

166 bringing Pluto to exact opposition of Neptune. Saturn is also square the Sun.

A final note on Hitler's natus.

Adolf = 38, bringing the ascendant (say 24 Libra) to the opposition of Neptune and Pluto in the 8th.

Hitler = 72, bringing ascendant to Moon–Jupiter.

Total, 110, ascendant to opposition Saturn, Saturn to opposition Neptune–Pluto.

But he reached great heights, materially speaking, and the same 110 brings Mars–Venus to trine Moon–Jupiter.

His sanity, at least latterly, may be in doubt, and 110 to Mercury makes it square Mars–Venus.

These are unusually strong configurations.

A hint at further possibilities.

The German word Tod (death) evaluates by the longer method at 39.

This brings the Fuehrer's ascendant to 3° Sagittarius.

At the time of his death his progressed Neptune was 2° 50′ Gemini.

This suggests that there are possibilities here of an entirely new method of rectification, as well as of general prediction.

So much for a glance into a field that some will reject with scorn and ridicule and others will find fascinating, and, it is hoped, illuminating.

It is, admittedly, a line of research wherein it is easy to be lost in a maze and to attribute wonderful results from what, critically examined, would turn out to be mere coincidence. It will be observed that these cases treat only of close aspects, perhaps up to an orb of 2°.

On the other hand it may be that in this direction will be found a true "Point of the Individual".

IX

SOME BRIEF STUDIES

THE ensuing are not designed to be detailed descriptions of nativities, but to be concise attempts at getting at the heart of the problem presented by each. For each nativity is a veritable riddle of the Sphinx, but some are more obscure than others. In some one seems to see a very open pathway; no definite choice has been made, and the native comes into life with many possibilities before him, or perhaps only the general possibility of living a useful, honest life in some ordinary occupation. In other cases it seems as if the key-note had been struck so often and so hard that the nativity gives it forth clearly, and even a casual glance shows what the work will be. Or, again, there may be several distinct tendencies, which the native will be called on to synthesise harmoniously.

In practical astrology it is often found that students are better at detail than at getting an idea of the real character of the native. They can say, perhaps, that a person will travel a lot, or will be sharp-tongued, or secretive, or amative, but whether he is a person of real principle with a few bad surface-habits, or a person of no principles except bad ones and perhaps some very agreeable manners—that, although far more important, they cannot always indicate. Of course, this is not strange, for many, if not most, people *are* of contradictory natures, rigidly moral, perhaps, in regard to money, but quite unprincipled with other forms of temptation, and so on. Nevertheless, we should seek to understand the basic matters first. If I ask an astrologer to advise me as to taking on, say, a new traveller, it is important that I should know what sort of manners he has; but even the externals of Lord Chesterfield will not be of much use to me if he has the faculty of always muddling accounts to his own advantage.

The following hints may be of use as a change from philosophy:

(1) *Principles*. The fixed-sign part of the horoscope has much to do with this part of the character. Study the Sun and Saturn, which are essentially of the fixed mode, and pay great attention to Venus and Jupiter, for few people who have them strong will lack good and honest intention. A bad ninth house is not a very encouraging sign. An afflicted Mercury does not necessarily mean dishonesty, but it seldom makes a person liked, which is another matter.

(2) *Morals*. Under this head I deal with habits, as apart from principles or settled convictions.

Judge these chiefly from the Water Triplicity, the Moon, Mars, and Venus, and the fifth and seventh houses. Remember that a prominent Saturn, even if afflicted, does not dispose to vice, for he is a timid influence, and, moreover, is never such a fool as not to see that "the devil is an ass".

(3) *Intelligence*. Under this term several aspects of mind may be considered. Cleverness, or "brain", may be judged primarily from bodies in the cadent houses and the common signs, for these always affect the mind. Usually if many bodies are in these parts of the map the native is quick-minded, intelligent, and mentally able. If they are well

configured then these powers work smoothly and successfully; if otherwise, then there are usually faults of expression.

Common sense, or horse-sense, is chiefly a matter of a good Saturn, but it is rarely deficient if any of the earthy signs are well tenanted.

Judgment, or what is often called intuition, i.e. the ability to form correct opinions without perceptible reasoning process, "at a glance" as it were, is chiefly a matter of a strong Jupiter.

Intellect, in the sense of a love of intellectual things, as distinct from intelligence, is related to the air-triplicity.

Power of expression, so often absent when there is great erudition, is mainly a matter of the cardinal signs and fire, as regards energy of deliverance, while felicitous phraseology is denoted by air and common signs.

(4) *Spirituality.* In the true sense, this will be found as a rule when air and fire and the benefic planets and Neptune are well tenanted, while negative signs and Mars, Saturn, and Uranus tend to materialism.

Beginners would do well to pay especial attention to the meaning of what I call *groupings* of planets. Neither in the radical horoscope nor by direction do isolated planets effect much; it is when we see powerful groups that big results are to be expected. For example, let an unaspected Mercury come to the square of the ascendant, and very little will occur. But let this planet be in square to Mars, so that this body comes, near the same time, to the opposition of the same point, and a very different result will appear; the period covered will be a clearly defined epoch in the life; and so generally.

CASE No. I

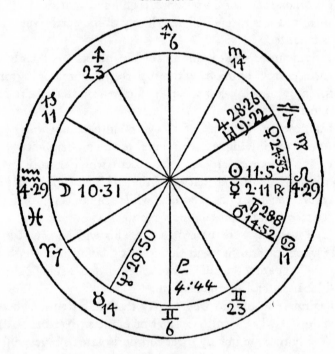

HOROSCOPE
OF
RUPERT BROOKE

Published in Modern Astrology, 1919, *p.* 141
Born at Rugby, at about 7.30 p.m., August 3rd, 1887

Note. The following symbols are used for brevity's sake: a = in aspect with, $\triangle$ = in good aspect with, $\boxminus$ = in bad aspect with.

I. Short-lived Genius: Rupert Brooke

Rupert Brooke died in the Gallipoli campaign as the result of a sunstroke.

In his nativity his genius as a poet is shown admirably by ♆ in the III ⚹ ☿ ♄ and △ ♀, while ☽ in asct. gives the powers of imagination which are common to all writers who use that faculty and which are usually shown horoscopically by lunar elements. Being in an airy sign, this faculty in Brooke's case was susceptible of careful training, but ☉ ♌ was sure to bestow true warmth of feeling which could never become unduly academised. ♀ in ♍ might incline perhaps to preciosity, but here again ☉ ♌ is a good protection.

The remainder of the map is less happy. ♃, part-ruler, is weak; ♅ is well configured with the lights and with ☿, but there is too much weight on the west side of the map and the position of the two malefics in ♋ in the VI is distinctly unfortunate, and might, I think, ultimately have done something to mar his poetical expression, for this house has distinct mental values. It is probably rare to find genuinely great poets—*Phoebo digna locuti*—with *any* planet markedly weak; for how can they deal adequately with life unless they can see it in all its aspects fairly and justly? This horoscope speaks rather of delicate and whimsical fancy.

However, it is a manly horoscope, and the good aspects of ♅ to the lights might have made the poet a very capable man of action. He was, indeed, far removed from the weaknesses that are usually ascribed to young poets. He possessed very unusual physical beauty, and this has often been ascribed to the 13th degrees of ♌ and ♒, near to his Sun and Moon.

To synthesise the polarity of ♌ ♒ through ♅ in ♎ might have been his work, but the two planets in the VIII □ the two in the VI disrupted the union of soul and body, although neither lights nor ascendant is violently afflicted, and most students would probably have foretold ill-health rather than death at an early age. One feels that in any case the horoscope was in some sense inferior to the man—there are strong factors and very weak ones, and the latter could not stand the stress, perhaps, of the former. We know but little as yet of the true causes of early death, and therefore we cannot easily see their stellar indications. At decease the "age along the Zodiac" was □ ♄ and ☍ ♃, the Point of Life being also with ♄, while ♅ was near ☍ asct.

CASE No. II

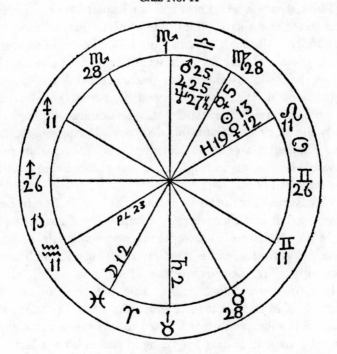

HOROSCOPE
OF
PERCY BYSSHE SHELLEY

From Notable Nativities

Born at Horsham, August 4th, 1792

NOTE: Since the above was first printed evidence has been adduced to the effect that Shelley was born under Aries.

II. Genius and Eccentricity: Percy Bysshe Shelley

This nativity is well known. Like Rupert Brooke, Shelley died young and abroad, but not until his genius had flowered plentifully. Although never accused, like Blake, of insanity, Shelley was certainly far from well-balanced, at any rate in youth, and while some of his unconventionalities such as vegetarianism, may be commended, others, such as his pamphlets on atheism, would still be admired by few. In early life he demonstrated his disapproval of primogeniture by foregoing a large inheritance (♄ ☌ IV), and from then onwards he was a true Neptunian, that planet being close to the meridian of his map.

Like Rupert Brooke and Tennyson, he had the Sun in Leo. His map falls into three distinct groups. The three bodies in ♎ in the IX, his ruler among them, represented air, and are the chief indicators of his intensely spiritual and intellectual mentality. The Leo group gave him his love of freedom, helped, of course by ♐ rising, and these also denote his warmth of heart and love of humanity. ☽ in ♓ strikes the same note more gently; it is hard to imagine a more sympathetic map, ☉ ♌ and ☽ ♓ being in particular a polarity of helpfulness and sympathy, while ♎ is a specially tender-hearted sign. ☿ △ ♄ is a much more practical element, but the latter planet falls under the ☍ ♆, as in Blake's horoscope, and Shelley does not seem ever to have felt this influence as one that made for practical common sense. He was, in fact, a true representative of the fire–air temperament.

Undoubtedly ♂ spoilt the best of the ♃ ☌ ♆, and ♀ ☌ ♅ acted strangely in his younger days, when he invited his discarded wife, in all kindness, to accompany him on his second "honeymoon" because she had always wanted to see Switzerland, or wherever he intended going!

Mars with his ruler, Uranus with the Sun, and Moon ⊟ the ♎︎ group terminated the life of this wild spirit, probably before he had learned to become a citizen of this plane. Some of his finest work, such as the closing stanzas of *Adonais*, reaches what would seem to be the highest imaginable expression of ♌︎–♎︎, while *The Cloud* is Jovian–Uranian, and again his political poems are ☉ ☌ ♅, an influence which in our days can probably be better expressed than in his, when there was but little of the nature of a *via media* between rigid convention and open rebellion.

Saturn on the Nadir was, with its opposition to Neptune, the keynote of Shelley's political attitude.

This is a nativity from which it is not at all difficult to judge genius or indeed anything else that is in fact true of the native. The two outer planets were almost equally strong; Uranus is with the Sun and Venus, which disposes of three important bodies. Neptune is on the M.C. with the ruler and disposes of the Moon, if we allow him Pisces as his own. The two planets governed his life and Neptune took him in death. Note that the two material planets are the two weakest, ♂ by sign and ♄ by mundane position.

G

III. Genius Allied to Madness: William Blake

Opinions have differed as to the sanity or otherwise of William Blake. The astrologer, seeing that he had ☿ and ♃, rulers of the III and IX, both in square to ♂, would naturally have good reason to conclude that he had at any rate very strange methods of expressing himself. The Moon, too, is involved in these afflictions by minor aspects, and the Sun scarcely escapes them. Neptune on the cusp of the II indicates, as it often does in this position, contempt for worldly success, and ♄ by opposition takes the native, so to speak, at his word and confirms him in poverty. This planet is, however, strong in ♒ and the lady of the XI is also strong: Blake received substantial help from friends.

The sublime genius of the man is shown by the exact ♀ ✶ ♅, by ☽ △ ♅, and by ☉ △ ♆. Uranus is in elevation in the IX and coloured all his work.

He was a supreme example of imagination in the literal sense of the word. To him all ideas, however abstract, assumed shape, and thus he was able to represent pictorially things which few indeed could visualise. Sometimes he descended, as we should think, from the sublime to the ridiculous, as when he portrayed the soul of a flea, an animal ruled by ☿, his weak planet. This imaginative faculty we can ascribe to the great preponderance of water; in Cancer, we said in Chapter II, the Divine Intellections take form, and so it was with the great mystic. The tender sympathies of Cancer are also beautifully expressed in some of the *Songs of Innocence*.

His love of prophetic writing is, of course, Sagittarian, and so, too, was his great independence of character.

His religious mysticism is quite in keeping with his fire—

CASE No. III

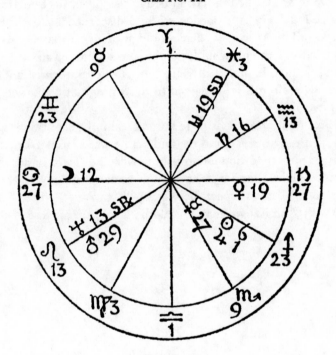

HOROSCOPE
OF
WILLIAM BLAKE

From Notable Nativities

Born in London, November 28th, 1757

water horoscope. Reason, called Urizen in his prophetic works, is to him a sort of Anti-Christ. Body he did not believe in at all. "Man has no body apart from his Soul, for that called Body is a portion of Soul discerned by the five senses." This is a view that would lead us to expect that the earthy element would not be prominent in his map. Venus is the sole planet therein, but its ruler Saturn is in air in ♒, wherein it is far removed from its pragmatic character as it ever is.

Blake was certainly as little immersed in physical things as any incarnate being could be, and yet he was a master-artist. This happy condition of lordship over the Two Lands is found, I believe, under ♋ as often as under any sign. In this case note the good aspects between ☽–♅ and ☉–♆ ; here ☿ is also with ♃ in its own sign, and both planets are in close △ to the asct.

NOTE: Pluto is about 19 ♐ in close square to Uranus, and this probably accentuated the love of the sombre and grotesque. Being in mutable signs it may have had much to do with his antipathy to reason.

CASE No. IV

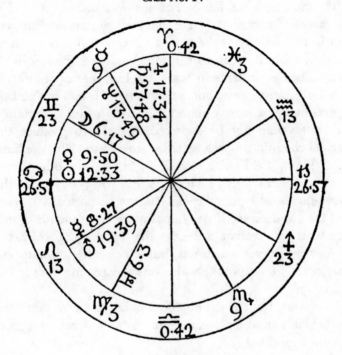

HOROSCOPE
OF
EMILY POPEJOY

From The Horoscope, *vol.* 1, *p.* 228

Born at Bagshot, 5.15 a.m., July 4th, 1880

Pluto is approximately 27½ ♉.

IV. DEATH FROM HARDSHIP AND ILL-TREATMENT

The horoscope of Emily Popejoy was published in *The Horoscope* and occasioned some comment, as it seemed strange that in the nativity of the poor girl, who died as a result of starvation and ill-treatment from her mistress, Jupiter holds the Midheaven in trine to Mars, the lord thereof. Saturn is also in the same house, but is nearer the XI, and has no bad aspects except a close square to the asct. which is certainly evil, but would not be expected, in itself to produce the tragical conditions which actually arose in the life. We have ☉ ∠ Pluto, ☿ ♂ □ ♆ and ☽ □ ♅, but on, the other hand there are good aspects, such as (☉ ☌ ♀) ✶ ♅ ✶ ♆. In the above-mentioned periodical a student is quoted as saying that the girl deserved little sympathy for being unable to survive with such a map, a remark the flippancy of which the writer very properly censures, but which reflects what most astrologers would probably think as regards the question of longevity.

Here was, from a theosophical point of view, a helpless soul which was, as it were, defeated by and driven back from the material plane.

Yet all the bodies are on the east of the map and six are in the south-east quadrant, positions which should have ensured a good deal of viability.

This is a case where the natus, by itself, would seem to reduce natal astrology to a very unsatisfactory condition.

Such cases do occur and it is right that we should take cognisance of this fact. We need not be unduly perturbed by it, for all sciences have their enigmas.

One explanation may be in the existence of undiscovered planets. The insertion of Pluto into this figure does not improve it, though neither can it be said to provide an adequate reason for the tragic denoument.

Another line of thought might be that the conditions that caused death are exactly such as might be expected from Saturn in close square to the ascendant from the Xth house. This often points to hardship and loneliness and stern or harsh treatment (cf. "A Human Document" in Leo's *Esoteric Astrology*). If it be said that, granting so much, it is still strange that the upshot was fatal, it might be replied that astrology deals only with general propensities, both of temperament and of fortune, and that from a given position one person may suffer severely and another but moderately.

Again, I have found that one really bad aspect from Uranus (in this case to the ruler) will often entirely upset an otherwise favourable nativity.

Further, the Sun is close to 75° from Saturn and this I believe to be a noteworthy bad aspect. That the evil happened under Sun square Saturn radical and progressed seems to indicate that this was actually the dangerous factor.

As for the sextiles of Neptune, I have never regarded the "good" aspects of this planet as worthy of reliance in matters of this world.

Note to the 1968 Edition

Reference to the preceding winter ingress goes far to explain the native's fate.

Inter alia there is an opposition Venus–Mars exactly on the natal Neptune.

CASE No. V

HOROSCOPE

OF

A NEURASTHENIC

Private sources

Born at Greenwich, 9 a.m., March 14th, 1863

Pluto is 9¾ ♉.

V. Psychological Defeat

We have here the nativity of an unfortunate man who developed fear of darkness—a common form of phobia. This, however, increased in such a manner as ultimately to become a general fear of life, so that business had to be abandoned and an existence of complete seclusion ensued, the native being incapable of facing things, or meeting the world on equal terms, or, indeed, on any terms at all.

The horoscope is rather difficult.

The Moon is in Capricorn, and it is δ cusp III, a position, whatever the planet, which indicates a certain degree of mental peculiarity. It is also □ ♀ in XII, a not very serious affliction. ♄ δ ♆ is serious, but ♂ is in mediation. Curiously we have such powerful benefic indications as ☿, ruler, △ ♃, and ♀ ✶ ♅. Except for a weak □ ♅ the Sun is without affliction. The M.C. is powerfully aspected, being △ ♂ ♄ ✶ ♆.

In general this would seem to be a XII house tragedy, as is indicated by the final complete withdrawal from the world. The Sun is in Pisces, and by the Campanus method of house-division (which I prefer but have not used in the diagrams because of its being unfamiliar to most students) both it, Neptune and Venus are in the XII house, Mercury being on the dividing-line between XI and XII. Neptune, one of the rulers of the natural XII house, has a very near opposition to Saturn, and this planet disposes of the Moon and the lord of the horoscope.

That Pluto, whose existence was unsuspected when this work was first written, has much to do with phobic conditions is hardly to be doubted. He rules that which is hidden but yet active; the impact and pressure of the unconscious upon the conscious. The fear of darkness was not without cause, whether we look for this in a past life or in some inherited memory of events that befell an ancestor. In this figure Pluto is in 9¾♉ in semi-square to the Sun and in close parallel with Neptune.

The trine of Mercury to Jupiter in air preserved the rational powers, though these could not dominate the pressure from the unconscious.

This map may be very usefully contrasted with the preceding. Fear is a problem of great interest, and both maps throw light upon it. It has, we may say, two astrological aspects. Cancer rules the instinct of self-preservation, and Capricorn what we must call, rather cumbrously, just appreciation of real values. Cancer feels fear, Capricorn knows that caution is necessary. The Moon and Saturn act similarly. One is subconscious, the other conscious.

In the girl's case the fear was very well justified, although there are, indeed, signs of psychological disease, as in ☿ □ ♆ and ☽ □ ♅ in mutables.

In Case No. V the worst aspect is from the cusp of the IX to the III, showing not only instinctual fear, but a panic element such as sufferers from these terrible ailments well know.

Why, then, is reason powerless against imagination, as, in such cases, it always is? In this instance the astrological answer is rather hard to find, for ☿ has △ ♃. But he is □ ♂ and ∠ ☽.

Once again the preceding winter ingress throws light upon this case, for Venus is in Capricorn 2, square Saturn–Neptune.

CASE NO. VI

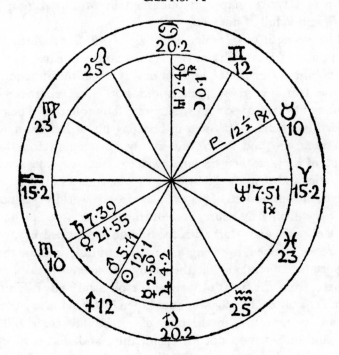

HOROSCOPE
OF
EDITH CAVELL

Published in Modern Astrology, 1916, *p.* 316

Born at Norwich, at 2.30 a.m., December 4th, 1865

VI. The Nativity of a Heroine

Nurse Cavell's map was published in *Modern Astrology*, 1916, and is full of interest.

The strength of ☿, which is ☌ ♃, of the Sun, which is △ ♆, and of ♄, which has two sextiles and two trines, show her nobility of character, and yet how is it that the afflictions of the two outermost planets did not affect character? Uranus has two oppositions, Neptune four squares. These, indeed, we believe operated in bringing about her betrayal and tragic end, and, for the rest, simply showed that, from the point of view of her personal welfare, she was too sympathetic, and took too great dangers; the squares of ♆ gave excess, the oppositions of ♅ gave what from a worldly point of view was foolhardy courage. Saturn gave her a compelling sense of duty, and Mars with the Sun abundant bravery.

Are we justified, in seeing a map such as this, to draw the important conclusion that the horoscope always speaks, as it were, from the point of view of the physical body? This, I think, is untenable, for we should then be forced to say that a bad configuration in the map of a criminal means only his punishment, and not his criminality, and that a lucky scamp, who "gets away with it", would have no afflictions at all. The converse would also be true, that good aspects mean only the happy results of our moral behaviour, so that a good man who meets constant misfortune would have nothing but bad aspects.

My belief is that Uranus and Neptune seldom, in themselves, injure the character severely. Their afflictions may, of course, show temperamental peculiarities; Nurse Cavell was probably highly strung, she may have been, from a practical point of view, rather inefficient (☿ □ ♆), though the

♐ positions would probably overcome this. The fact remains that she was a rare example of sympathy and fortitude, of which virtues her map bears eloquent testimony. While many elements indicate these traits, it is as a Saturn–Scorpio heroine that she is, I think, pre-eminent.

Hers is a case directly opposite to the two foregoing. Her soul was indeed in conflict with the world, but most decisively overcame it. Mars is purified by the trine of Neptune, Saturn by its several good aspects, but in particular by Jupiter; and before her death even the separative forces of Uranus were dissolved through the conquest of the opposition of that planet to Jupiter.

The powers of the evil aspects to bind this soul in matter through fear were completely defeated, and the essential prepotency of the spirit over all limitation was gloriously vindicated.

This nativity may be contrasted with that of Nietzsche,[1] who had also had ☿ ☍ ♅ at the beginning of cardinal signs, in his case, the two positives. His Moon was in ♐ near Nurse Cavell's ☉, and his ☉ was in ♎ near her ascendant, and, like hers, △ ♆.

He, too, was a sympathetic man, who nursed the wounded in the war of 1871; and, just as Saturn mediated Nurse Cavell's oppositions, so, in ♒, did it also in his case. Both were meant for stern work, and (except through her sign ♎) each had ♀ rather weakly placed. ♂ ⚻ ☿ ♃, both lords of the common cross, signifies Nietzsche's mental downfall; and his grandiose conception of the superman was based on the erroneous and, indeed, logically absurd belief that the world could be conquered by material forces embodied in man, i.e. by itself. This is shown by the condition in his nativity of

[1] Born October 15th, 1844, 0½ ♐ rising.

the three spiritual planets, ♃ spoilt by ☍ ♂, ♀ without powerful aspects and weak by sign, and ♆ indeed △ ☉, but ∠ ♅
and ⊡ ☿, as well as ☐ asct. On the other hand, ♂, ♄, ♅ are
powerfully conjoined, and, so to speak, hold ☿ in their grasp.
♄ is indeed strong, but there is a dissociate ☐ ☉. This map
is that of one who would deny the truth of the words "Not by
might nor by power, but by My spirit . . ."

CASE No. VII

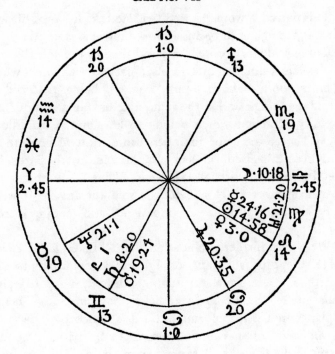

HOROSCOPE
OF
WOULD-BE SUICIDE

Private sources

Born in Holland, 9 p.m., August 7th, 1883

VII. SUICIDAL TENDENCIES

This native, a woman, tried twice to take her own life and died at the age of forty-one from a lung complaint.

Three malefics are in II around the cusp of the III, and ♂ is violently afflicted by Uranus, a paradoxical planet which operates both "above" and "below", being powerful in mundane things, and at the same time having a breadth and rapidity of action which belong to less limited conditions. Hence he is apt to be impatient, intolerant of hindrances, and, in certain circumstances, unable to endure the Saturnian conditions of terrestrial existence. Thus he becomes the planet of one type of suicide, the soul turning, as it were, upon the body in a fury of impatience and rending it from itself.

We obtain further explanation from ♆ □ ☉ ☿ and ♂ cusp VIII. Neptune is a planet of high standards; it may be said to come down from spiritual conditions, and, to speak colloquially, to expect a lot of life and of mankind. Though a planet that is full of sympathy, it is noticeable how often its afflicted action causes a person to be critical; nobody seems to do as well as it expects them to do. This condition often remains until the native has gained some enlightenment as to the nature of mundane existence and the reasons for the common shortcomings of humanity.

In this case the tendency of Neptune to drift away from material things has caused the native to seek the freedom of a larger life by the wrong means of premature and deliberate death. And yet, with characteristic elusiveness, the planet frustrated the very tendency it caused.

This map indicates a withdrawal and shrinking from

material conditions, into contact with which the ♂ ascendant has nevertheless forced it.

The death from lung-disease points to the fact that the malefics in the 3rd sign and around the third house were the chief point of stress.

CASE No. VIII

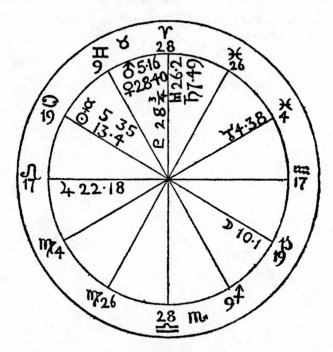

HOROSCOPE
OF
WILLIAM T. STEAD

From Notable Nativities

Born July 5th, 1849, in Co. Durham

VIII. A Man of Courage

We must thus describe William Stead, whose rising Jupiter, in Leo, made him a truly leonine man in appearance and character.

The horoscope is chosen chiefly for its admirable exemplification of what is meant by horoscopic grouping. We have one group of the two Lights, in opposition, and Saturn in square to both. Again we have ☿ △ ♆ with ♂ ✳ each, this group being partly joined with the first, by wide orbs. Thirdly, we have ♃ △ ♅, and, fourthly, ♀ □ ♆ on cusp VIII.

Of these groups the first is mainly concerned with destiny. Stead struggled hard and lost heavily; finally, he lost his life. He was doomed to be at loggerheads with materialism and the elements in society which are specially related, by analogy, to the material plane, such as conservatism, entrenched authority, and obsolete laws. But, with his Viking ascendant, he was meant to fight his antagonist to the last and ask no quarter.

His journalistic ability and his devotion to the cause of peace and disarmament come under the second group, in which ☿ is brilliantly configured, though □ ♄. ☿ △ ♆ is common in successful publicists, but □ ♄ spelt heavy loss.

All sorts of things contributed to his spiritualistic experiences and beliefs. We may credit ♃ △ ♅ with some of these, but ♄ in IX must be held responsible for their less profound aspects and for the fact (as I believe) that the native was not attracted to a more philosophic interest in occultism.

As regards the place of Pluto, on the mid-heaven and in close conjunction with Uranus, this can be connected with the native's spiritism and also with his love of bringing hidden scandals and abuses to light by unconventional means.

The episode of the "Maiden Tribute" falls in particular under ♀ □ ♆.[1] Here, as in Nurse Cavell's case, the bad aspect does not reflect on the character, but may be taken as indicative of the obloquy and unpleasantness which were incurred, and possibly of the peculiar method Stead employed. He used to celebrate his sentence by donning convict clothes on the anniversaries of his release, which appears to me to be a foolish eccentricity due, I suppose, to Uranus on the meridian, and to the sensationalism of distorted Cancerian influences.

Cancer and Leo might easily display what are known in these days as exhibitionist tendencies.

[1] In order to draw attention to the alleged common traffic in young girls for immoral purposes, Stead actually "procured" a girl of 13 or thereabouts, in a technical sense only of course, and suffered imprisonment in consequence.

CASE No. IX

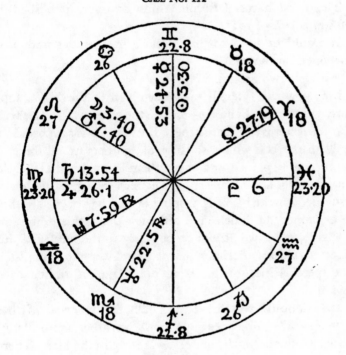

HOROSCOPE
OF
RALPH WALDO EMERSON

Published in Modern Astrology, 1921, *p.* 277

Born at Boston, Mass., May 25th, 1803, map cast for 1 hr. 16 min.,
local time

IX. A Great Philosopher

This is the natus of Ralph Waldo Emerson, published in *Modern Astrology*, 1921.

It would be hard to find a more harmonious and proportioned horoscope.

We have two groups.

Mercury, the ruler, is in its own sign in the M.C., supported on the one hand by ♀ and on the other by ♃. It is true that the latter is in square aspect, but it again is supported by ✶ ♅ in the III, which, so to speak, gathers up all three of the preceding planets and passes them through the III. I do not know enough of Emerson's writings to suggest with any assurance how the ☿ ☐ ♃ worked out; it has been said that he explained too much, and although this seems to me improbable, yet it would not be contrary to the nature of this aspect to do so. Perhaps his philosophy is too optimistic. The peculiarities of his style are Uranian rather than Jovian.

It is doubtful whether Saturn falls in this group; it has little special significance, and perhaps rather more of this planet's influence is the one thing lacking in the map. There are no bodies in either ♑ or ♒.

The second group begins with the Sun, passing to the sextile of the conjunction of Moon and Mars, and thence to the grand completion of Uranus, in trine with the Sun and in sextile to the other two. A more splendid configuration cannot be imagined. It shows the rarest harmony of intellect and emotion.

We see that, with the possible exception of Saturn, these two groups include all the planets, the ascendant, and Midheaven. One must regard this as a truly integral horoscope, probably marking almost the highest development of man that can be astrologically pictured.

Note how the strong ☿ element is softened and expanded by the rising ♃ and vitalised by the Leo planets, while in turn these are intellectualised by ☿.

CASE No. X

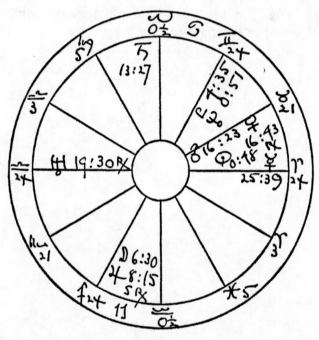

HOROSCOPE
OF
ADOLF HITLER

Born 13° East, 48° North, at about 6 hrs. 17 mins. p.m., local time,
on April 20th, 1889

X. A Maniac Genius

It is probable that the natus of Adolf Hitler would exemplify the Law of Subsumption to which we have referred in a most striking manner, had we the horoscopes to which to relate it.

For surely the most remarkable thing about this man was not what we see in him personally but in the power he wielded over others.

There is nothing so very unusual in a man's being inordinately ambitious and quite unrelenting and unflinching in the execution of his plans for his own and his nation's aggrandizement. He must have possessed considerable military talents, but that, again, is not very rare.

He had a remarkable, but quite unbalanced, mind.

What he had was a unique power of influencing others, and this, one feels, must have been indicated, astrologically, not so much by his own nativity as by its relations with the map, quite unknown, of his race. In a word, he was not so much an individual ego *per se* as the focus-point of mighty cosmic forces.

Thus, the Jupiter–Saturn conjunction prior to his birth fell, on April 18th, 1881, within a degree of his natal Sun. Not an outstanding feature in itself and equally applicable to many. But in the great mutation figure of 1842 the conjunction falls in 8° 54′ Capricorn, near his Moon and Jupiter. Moreover, if we look at this chart as it appeared for his birth-place, his natal Moon and Jupiter are just rising, and his Venus–Mars conjunction is close to the southern meridian.

Further research would doubtless reveal many such correlations.

The cosmic nature of the figure of birth is made plain, I think, if we look at it zodiacally, forgetting the houses, or, if this makes it clearer, putting 0° Aries on the ascendant.

We then see Mercury in the 1st "house", indicative of a man whose influence was so largely through his book and his speeches.

Three bodies are in Taurus, indicating the architectural and generally constructive direction of the ego. Hitler dreamed of building a Reich that would last a thousand years. Basically he was not destructive; his destructions were designed to be a clearing of the site for a great construction. Materially, he accumulated great wealth as well as achieving immense power, both expressions of the Taurus ideal.

Then come Pluto and Neptune on "cusp 3", denoting as clearly as anything could his demoniac nature and notorious "intuitions".

Saturn in the 5th sign often shows childlessness and in the case of Hitler it is afflicted. The whole life was barren and left only desolation behind it.

Uranus is in the 7th sign.

Next, Moon and Jupiter conjoined on the zodiacal 10th.

It seems that the nature of the man—or perhaps we should rather say, his cosmic significance—is far more apparent from his zodiacal study than from his geniture erected in the usual manner.

Hitler, for good or evil, lifted himself above the circumscribing Houses into cosmic values.

The fact that many thousands must have had virtually identical zodiacal maps is not a valid argument against this approach to his nativity or those of others like him. He belonged to a race apart from ordinary individuals, to those men and women chosen, it would seem, to work out some cosmic purpose beyond our ken and sometimes involving the cruellest sufferings in its unfoldment.

INDEX

Better books make better astrologers.
Here are some of our other titles:

AstroAmerica's Daily Ephemeris, 2010-2020
AstroAmerica's Daily Ephemeris, 2000-2020
  - both for Midnight. Compiled & formatted by David R. Roell

Al Biruni
The Book of Instructions in the Elements of the Art of Astrology,
  1029 AD, translated by R. Ramsay Wright

Derek Appleby
Horary Astrology: The Art of Astrological Divination

E. H. Bailey
The Prenatal Epoch

Joseph Blagrave
Astrological Practice of Physick

C.E.O. Carter
The Astrology of Accidents
An Encyclopaedia of Psychological Astrology
Essays on the Foundations of Astrology
The Principles of Astrology, *Intermediate no. 1*
Some Principles of Horoscopic Delineation, *Intermediate no. 2*
Symbolic Directions in Modern Astrology

Charubel & Sepharial
Degrees of the Zodiac Symbolized, *1898*

Nicholas Culpeper
Astrological Judgement of Diseases from the Decumbiture of the
  Sick, *1655, and,* **Urinalia,** *1658*

Dorotheus of Sidon
Carmen Astrologicum, *c. 50 AD, translated by David Pingree*

Nicholas deVore
Encyclopedia of Astrology

Firmicus Maternus
Ancient Astrology Theory & Practice: Matheseos Libri VIII,
c. 350 AD, translated by Jean Rhys Bram

William Lilly
Christian Astrology, books 1 & 2, *1647*
  The Introduction to Astrology, Resolution of all manner of questions.
Christian Astrology, book 3, *1647*
  Easie and plaine method teaching how to judge upon nativities.

CPSIA information can be obtained at www.ICGtesting.com
Printed in the USA
LVOW12s1953171113

361625LV00001B/78/P